A Dream, a Rock, and a Pillar of Fire

PROCEEDINGS of the
MORMON THEOLOGY SEMINAR

The PROCEEDINGS OF THE MORMON THEOLOGY SEMINAR series is based on a novel idea: that Mormons do theology. Doing theology is different from weighing history or deciding doctrine. Theology speculates. It experiments with questions and advances hypotheses. It tests new angles and pulls loose threads.

The Mormon Theology Seminar organizes interdisciplinary, collaborative, theological readings of Latter-day Saint scripture. Seminar participants with diverse backgrounds closely explore familiar texts in creative ways. In partnership with the Laura F. Willes Center for Book of Mormon Studies at the Neal A. Maxwell Institute for Religious Scholarship, the Mormon Theology Seminar presents these experiments upon the word to foster greater theological engagement with basic Mormon texts.

Series Editor
Brian M. Hauglid

Other MORMON THEOLOGY SEMINAR *books include:*
Adam S. Miller, ed.,
An Experiment on the Word: Reading Alma 32

Joseph M. Spencer and Jenny Webb, eds.,
Reading Nephi Reading Isaiah: 2 Nephi 26–27

Julie M. Smith, ed.,
Apocalypse: Reading Revelation 21–22

Jeremiah John and Joseph M. Spencer, eds.,
Embracing the Law: Reading Doctrine and Covenants 42

Adam S. Miller, ed.,
Fleeing the Garden: Reading Genesis 2–3

mi.byu.edu/pmts

A Dream, a Rock, and a Pillar of Fire

Reading 1 Nephi 1

Edited by
Adam S. Miller

NEAL A. MAXWELL
INSTITUTE *for*
RELIGIOUS SCHOLARSHIP

Brigham Young University
Provo, Utah

A Proceedings of the Mormon Theology Seminar book

Neal A. Maxwell Institute, Provo 84602 | maxwellinstitute.byu.edu

Library of Congress Cataloging-in-Publication Data

Names: Mormon Theology Seminar (2014 : London, England), author. | Miller, Adam S., editor. | Mormon Theology Seminar. Proceedings of the Mormon Theology Seminar
Title: A dream, a rock, and a pillar of fire : reading 1 Nephi 1 / edited by Adam S. Miller.
Description: Provo, Utah : Neal A. Maxwell Institute, Brigham Young University / [2017] | Includes bibliographical references.
Identifiers: LCCN 2017032610 (print) | LCCN 2017036002 (ebook) | ISBN 9780842530132 (ePub) | ISBN 9780842530149 (Kindle) | ISBN 9780842530125 (print : alk. paper)
Subjects: LCSH: Book of Mormon. Nephi, 1st—Congresses. | Church of Jesus Christ of Latter-day Saints—Doctrines—Congresses. | Mormon Church—Doctrines—Congresses.
Classification: LCC BX8627 (ebook) | LCC BX8627 .M67 2014 (print) | DDC 289.3/22—dc23
LC record available at https://lccn.loc.gov/2017032610

∞ This paper meets the requirements of ANSI/NISO z39.48-1992 (Permanence of Paper).

ISBN 978-0-8425-3012-5

Cover and book design: Jenny Webb and Andrew Heiss

Printed in the United States of America

Contents

Acknowledgments

OUR THANKS TO BRIAN HAUGLID and the Laura F. Willes Center for Book of Mormon Studies, the Neal A. Maxwell Institute for Religious Scholarship, and James E. Faulconer as a Richard L. Evans Chair of Religious Understanding at Brigham Young University for their generous support of the Mormon Theology Seminar. Without their support, the live, two-week format for the seminar would not be possible. More, a special thanks to Brigham Young University's London Centre and James E. Faulconer for their willingness to host this Mormon Theology Seminar on 1 Nephi 1.

Introduction

For as long as I can remember, I've wanted to build something big. But right from the start this impulse took less practical forms. Rather than framing houses or designing cars, I set my heart on making books. And more than just wanting to write books, my attention fixed on building a kind of collaborative machine that would itself make many, many books. I wanted shelves full of books. I wanted books by the yard. I wanted a project that would work on a scale of decades rather than days and that could, as a result, matter for a hundred years. The Mormon Theology Seminar is one product of this impulse. And this seminar in particular, *A Dream, a Rock, and a Pillar of Fire: Reading 1 Nephi 1*, marks a tipping point in the pursuit of that goal.

Any success on this scale requires more than work. It requires talented partners and a measure of good luck. In 2006, during my second year as a philosophy professor at Collin College, I got a note from Joseph Spencer. Spencer, whom I had never met, was a former student of James Faulconer, a friend and philosophy professor at Brigham Young University. Spencer wanted to start an email list called LDS-HERM. The idea was to create a space where big, brawling, technical discussions of phenomenology and hermeneutics could cross-pollinate with Mormon ideas. The list was a potent incubator for new ideas. Unfolding over a couple of years, those early discussions generated a lot of heat and light. More, they welded us together as friends. Apart from the handful of people on that list, who else would spend months with any one of us talking about Jacques Lacan and the sealing power, Martin Heidegger and the nature of revelation, or Alain Badiou on St. Paul?

But these private discussions only whetted our appetite. Soon, we wanted to try something bigger, something formal and public. This led to a beta version of the Mormon Theology Seminar in 2007. We piloted a seven-month online seminar focused on Abraham that offered close, collaborative, theological readings of the Abraham narratives in Genesis, the Book of Abraham, Søren Kierkegaard's *Fear and Trembling*, and Jacques Derrida's *The Gift of Death*. Seven people participated, but the project, though beautiful, turned out to be too ambitious by half.

For a second try, we narrowed the scope of the seminar to just a single chapter of scripture, dropped the philosophy readings, and contracted the scale of time. Robert Couch, James Faulconer, Julie Smith, Joseph Spencer, Jenny Webb, and I then spent three months online reading Alma 32 together, working through the text word by word, line by line, verse by verse. This version of the seminar was a substantial success. It culminated in a public conference at BYU in 2008, and its participants formed the core group that to this day serve as the seminar's executive board.

We wanted then to find a publisher for this collection of conference papers. Knowing that the project was too narrow for a typical academic press and too scholarly for a trade press, we tried Brigham Young University's Neal A. Maxwell Institute for Religious Scholarship. But the timing was wrong. Empowered by the revolution in print-on-demand books, we plunged ahead and founded an independent academic press of our own. With this press, we wanted to stake out ground for the kind of work we were doing at the intersection of theory and scripture, and we wanted to offer solid evidence that, in practice, our approach was not only possible but potent. Thus, Salt Press was born. Co-owned by Robert Couch, Joseph Spencer, Jenny Webb, and myself, Salt Press opened for business in 2009.

In December 2011, Salt Press published the proceedings of that first Mormon Theology Seminar as *An Experiment on the Word: Reading Alma 32*. It simultaneously published those of our second seminar,

Reading Nephi Reading Isaiah: 2 Nephi 26–27. One month later, in January 2012, Salt also published the first edition of Spencer's book, *An Other Testament: On Typology*. Four more online seminars with a variety of new participants were held over the next few years, addressing Doctrine and Covenants 42, Revelation 21–22, 2 Nephi 2, and Genesis 2–3. Proceedings from most of these seminars, together with a number of other solicited titles and submitted monographs, were to be forthcoming.

However, in March 2013, the Maxwell Institute approached Salt Press with an offer. Sold on the work that Salt Press had managed to do on its own, the Institute's pitch was straightforward: we have resources and you have content. Let Maxwell take over the resource-intensive work of actually publishing and distributing the kind of content you've championed, and you can return your full attention to the work of creating and soliciting that same kind of content. In response, we happily handed over our current and planned publications.

More, the Institute agreed to partner with the Mormon Theology Seminar to sponsor future seminars that would adapt our online model for a live, two-week format. These live seminars would be directed by Spencer and myself and would look to build long-term relationships with a variety of non-Mormon host institutions like Union Theological Seminary in New York, New York, and the Graduate Theological Union in Berkeley, California. As part of this effort, Brian Hauglid and the Laura F. Willes Center for Book of Mormon Studies, housed in the Maxwell Institute, stepped in to fund and help organize future seminars.

In June 2014, hosted by Faulconer at BYU's London Centre, the first live, two-week version of the seminar convened. In addition to Spencer and myself, five other scholars from a variety of disciplinary backgrounds participated: George Handley (humanities), Benjamin Peters (media studies), Julie Smith (New Testament studies), Michaël Ulrich (mathematics), and Miranda Wilcox (English). Initially a little nervous that the twenty assigned verses from 1 Nephi 1 might not offer enough material to occupy our collective attention for two weeks, we were instead scrambling by the third day to even skim through the handful of verses assigned for that five hours of discussion. Questions, angles, and hypotheses seemed to grow exponentially as observations, intertextual connections, insights, and theological ramifications fed off of each other. The seminar's collaboratively written "summary report" attempts to capture some of the central themes that recurred throughout these discussions, but each of the individually written papers, while clearly sharing this common background, eventually goes its own way in pursuit of its own themes.

Julie Smith's paper, "Huldah's Long Shadow," helps provide crucial historical background for 1 Nephi 1 by examining the role played by King Josiah's sweeping religious reforms in setting the stage for Lehi's Jerusalem some twenty-five years later. In particular, Smith compares and contrasts Huldah, a prophetess central to those reforms, and Lehi.

My own paper, "Burnt Offerings: Favor, Afflictions, and the Mysteries of God," contrasts the accounts given of Lehi's two inaugural visions as reported by Nephi. The first vision is raw and elemental, focused on rock and fire. The second vision, in contrast, unfolds as a throne theophany that pivots around the reception and reading of a revealed text. Taking these visions as touchstones, I ask what they may teach about the nature of revelation, suffering, and salvation.

In "Dreams, Visions, and Foolish Imaginations: Alternative History as Sacred History in the Book of Mormon," George Handley reads 1 Nephi 1 with an eye to the "counterhistory" that, rather than being directly presented by Nephi's written record, is instead only implied by the lingering traces of what Nephi chose *not* to include in his abridgment. Reflecting, then, on the role played by what goes unnoticed and unsaid in 1 Nephi 1, Handley asks about the role such counterhistories may play in our own experiences of revelation and redemption.

With his paper, "Potent Messianism: Textual, Historical, and Theological Notes on 1 Nephi 1:18–20," Joseph Spencer investigates the different reactions reported by Nephi in response to Lehi's distinct prophetic messages. When Lehi prophesies that Jerusalem will be destroyed, the people laugh. But when he prophesies that a Messiah will come, the people try to kill him. Drawing on a close reading of the verses involved and additional information about the historical background against which Lehi's message would have been received,

Spencer suggests some general conclusions that might be drawn about the dangers of proclaiming the Messiah's advent.

Miranda Wilcox offers a textual history of the phrase *tender mercies* in 1 Nephi 1:20 in "*Tender Mercies* in English Scriptural Idiom and in Nephi's Record." Noting that the phrase has recently come to resonate in a very specific way for contemporary Latter-day Saints, Wilcox traces this English rendition back to its biblical roots in the Psalms and then through various stages of transformation as different translation projects develop its use in the English language.

Michaël Ulrich's paper, "Joining the Heavenly Chorus," focuses on the throne theophany described in Lehi's second vision in 1 Nephi 1. Paying particular attention to the role of the "heavenly chorus" in this theophany, Ulrich develops a comparative analysis of this vision with Lehi's more famous vision of the tree of life in 1 Nephi 8 and argues that the former vision may be, in some respects, a key to understanding the latter.

"The Missing Medium: Rereading Revelation as Interruption in 1 Nephi 1," written by Benjamin Peters, rounds out this volume's collection of essays. Peters notes a number of key moments in 1 Nephi 1 when, rather than proceeding to directly and emphatically reveal what one would expect, the narrative is instead interrupted and redirected. Peters then develops a model of revelation that takes these interruptions and misdirections into account as an essential feature of revelation rather than simply treating it as a failure of that revelatory process.

In addition to this collection of seminar papers, past and future volumes in the proceedings of the Mormon Theology Seminar will now be published with the Maxwell Institute. Our shared hope is that this partnership will be productive for many years as scholarly interest in Mormon texts and Mormon ideas continues to grow. For my part, my hope is that the Mormon Theology Seminar will itself leave for future generations whole shelves full of such books.

—Adam S. Miller

Summary Report

Question 1: What political and religious contexts are relevant to understanding 1 Nephi 1? Who are the "many prophets" referenced in verse 4? For Lehi, what might a contemporary understanding of "a messiah" have looked like?

THE POLITICAL CONTEXT OF 1 NEPHI 1 is complex and, for Judah, precarious. Assyrian domination of the region was coming to an end as Babylonian strength increased. The Assyrian decline led to unrest as Babylon and Egypt fought for control of Judah. Jerusalem eventually fell to the Babylonians (see 2 Kings 24–25). This resulted in the installation of Zedekiah as something of a Babylonian puppet king in 597 BCE (see 1 Nephi 1:4).

The reforms of King Josiah (see 2 Kings 22 and 2 Chronicles 34) in 622 BCE provide the most important religious context for 1 Nephi 1. Josiah's efforts to refurbish the temple led to the discovery of a lost scroll that apparently contained something akin to the book of Deuteronomy. The prophetess Huldah proclaimed the word of the Lord in relation to this lost text, and in response, Josiah purged the temple of idols and reinstituted the celebration of Passover. These dramatic reformations, taking place in Lehi's own lifetime, would have profoundly shaped Lehi's own religious experience.

Adding to this context, 1 Nephi 1:4 refers to "many prophets."[1] The group who lived during the time might include some of the prophets whose names are known from the Hebrew Bible, including Zephaniah (see Zephaniah 1:1), Jeremiah (see Jeremiah 1:1), Huldah (see 2 Kings 22:14), Nahum (see Nahum 1:1), Daniel (see Daniel 1:6), Ezekiel (see Ezekiel 1:3), and Urijah (Jeremiah 26:20). Of course, this verse could also include others who go unmentioned. Clearly, the definition of *prophet* in these verses differs from the modern Latter-day Saint understanding, which permits but one prophet, or president, at a time. Having multiple prophets in this context indicates that they filled a different role—one that, rather than being executive, centered on their call to preach and write.

Similarly, the use of the term *messiah* in 1 Nephi 1 may depart in some ways from modern expectations. The word *messiah* first occurs in the Book of Mormon in 1 Nephi 1:19, where Lehi preaches about "the coming of a Messiah." Though modern readers are accustomed to think almost exclusively about Jesus Christ as the Messiah, here the indefinite article speaks of *a* messiah and not of *the* Messiah. The use of an indefinite article at this early point in the narrative raises questions about how much Lehi then understood about who or what the Messiah would be.

Our English word *messiah* comes from the Hebrew *māšîaḥ*, meaning "anointed one." It shares the same basic meaning as the Greek term *Christ*. A messiah is a person who has been called of God to perform a particular task or mission. In these general terms, the Bible refers to a number of individuals beside Jesus Christ as messiahs. For example, Cyrus, king of Persia, is called "[my] anointed" by the Lord in Isaiah 45:1, and the kings of Israel—including Saul (1 Samuel 24:6) and David (2 Samuel 22:51)—are called "anointed." While some references to a

---

1. Throughout this volume, we have used Royal Skousen's *The Book of Mormon: The Earliest Text* (New Haven: Yale University Press, 2009) for our base text, providing a note wherever we have used another edition.

messiah in the Old Testament seem to refer directly to Jesus Christ, it is difficult to determine how clearly people at the time understood the specifics of Christ's mission.

What might Lehi have understood by the term *messiah* at the time he received the visions recounted by Nephi in 1 Nephi 1? Passages of Hebrew scripture, like 1 Samuel 2:10, emphasize a messiah as one full of power and might: "And he shall give strength unto his king, and exalt the horn of his anointed." It could be that Lehi first understood the promise of a messiah in this more general and political way. Lehi's visions and preaching, as Nephi recounts them, are tightly focused on the destruction of Jerusalem, the captivity of the Jewish people in Babylon, and the possibility of their collective redemption from captivity.

Regardless, Nephi's editorial choice to retain what was likely his father's own use of the indefinite article with respect to the "coming of a Messiah" is intriguing. This choice indicates that a careful, diachronic examination of the Nephite understanding of Christ's person and mission—in both Nephi's record and the Book of Mormon as a whole—could yield rich returns.

Question 2: What does Nephi's heavy editorial presence in 1 Nephi 1 say about the nature of his project? How does this presence shape our understanding of who Nephi is? What anxieties might this heavy editorial presence disclose?

When compared with the opening words of the Bible, the opening words of the Book of Mormon betray an explicit obsession with authorship. In Genesis, the narrative lacks self-reference, and it never announces a specific plan for the story it intends to tell. Nephi, on the other hand, consistently interrupts his narrative with notes about his own peculiar circumstances, his inspired intentions for the record, his hopes for his readers, and his worries about whether he can fulfill his authorial responsibilities. The result is an unusual text for scripture. As readers, we not only know who the author of the text is, we hear him speak in personal terms and directly address the reader with a second-person "you"—though it is not clear at the outset of the record who that "you" is (see 1 Nephi 1:20).

In 1 Nephi 1, Nephi often shifts from narrative report to editorial address. He tells us who he and his family are (v. 1). He tells us about his education, including his language and culture (vv. 1–2). He tells us of his difficulties, but also of the divine favor he has experienced (v. 1). He insists that he is the one who personally made this record (vv. 1, 3, 16–18). He reports on his intention to abridge his father's writings and provides a basic outline of the whole of his first book (vv. 16–17). He tells his readers in advance what he hopes to show them (vv. 1, 20) and emphasizes what he wants them to know (v. 18). And he testifies that what he means to show his readers is based on firsthand experience (v. 3). That Nephi insists on saying so much about himself and his intentions is, in some ways, as instructive as what Nephi actually says in his editorial asides.

Nephi is deeply concerned with his work as an author and acutely anxious about its being received in the right way. Presumably some of Nephi's anxiety derives from his knowledge of the prophetic tradition (he knows the writings of Isaiah and, probably, Jeremiah). Nephi seems anxious to put himself into relation with and yet keep a certain distance from that tradition. In Isaiah and Jeremiah, the writings of the prophets begin with a clear formula: "The word of the Lord unto…" But Nephi avoids this standard formula. Betraying his concern about the relationship between his book and theirs and wanting to convince us that he is no prophetic usurper, Nephi begins instead with "I, Nephi…" It is possible to read Nephi's work as originally being written for his children and only later becoming a book of prophecy. In the first place, then, 1 Nephi 1 is originally more a record for the Lamanites and Nephites than it is for us.

However we read the first chapter's opening, the shift at its conclusion—from a kind of family history to a testimony of the Messiah—retroactively changes the book's beginning. Even if Nephi sets out to write family history, the entire book ends up becoming a testimony of a messiah-to-come. With this retroaction, what has been Nephi's anxiety about his own reputation and extended family is transformed into anxiety about his standing as a prophet and about the souls of his readers.

It becomes the anxiety proper to a prophet trying to fulfill his commission, not just the anxiety of a grandfather hoping to help children and great-grandchildren.

Nephi's original anxiety, though, is not out of place. As a refugee and immigrant to an unfamiliar world, Nephi is reasonably concerned about his identity and how to pass on that sense of identity to his children. Even living in Jerusalem, he was out of place: a northern tribesman living in the area of the southern tribes. In the New World, he has been separated even from that immigrant identity.

Finally, it is important to remember that 1 Nephi 1 is not the beginning Mormon intended for the Book of Mormon. It became the beginning only because Mormon's chosen beginning (Lehi's "116 pages") was lost. That bit of reshuffling forcefully reminds us that there is, inevitably, a human element at work in scripture. This same reminder echoes in Nephi's own opening words: "I, Nephi." The Book of Mormon—as we have it—thus opens with its human dimension doubly emphasized.

Question 3: Why, in his account of his father's visions, does Nephi repeatedly defer and displace crucial information about his father's call and the content of his father's revelations? What might this tendency toward deferral and displacement say, in general, about the role of written texts in revelation? What might it say, in particular, about the role of the Book of Mormon?

First Nephi 1 raises difficult questions about why crucial information is often deferred or displaced in our inspired records, and it raises these questions on a number of levels. Nephi's explicit announcement that his record will select, omit, and abridge prompts a consideration of the general role of selection and omission in revelation, and more, it prompts a reconsideration of the role played by the missing plates from which Joseph Smith initially translated the text of the Book of Mormon.

Nephi admits up front that he will not be telling us everything: "And now I Nephi, do not make a full account of the things which my father hath written" (1 Nephi 1:16). Further, he explains that his purposeful selections are guided by his desire to summarize "the things of God. For the fullness of mine intent is that I may persuade men to come unto the God of Abraham" (1 Nephi 6:3–4). Thus, we are told that his selections and omissions have something to do with his broader purpose in writing a sacred history that will have a powerful effect on his readers. Are redaction and abridgment necessary to this effect? Would omitted details have been merely extraneous? Or were they left aside reluctantly because of the burden involved in engraving the plates?

A close look at the first chapter showcases this problem. Without access to the lost book of Lehi or the original plates, it is impossible to determine with precision the meaning of Nephi's selections and redactions. For example, given what Nephi does tell us, we are left to wonder where Lehi is going in such a hurry as he prays on behalf of his people (1 Nephi 1:5). Having heard the prophets cry repentance, is he going to repent? If so, where? Why are we told so little about what he "saw and heard" in his first vision (v. 6)? And why, when Lehi does have a chance to converse with the "one" who descends from heaven, does the "one" give Lehi a book to read instead of speaking to him directly (vv. 9–11)?

Nephi's accounts of these visions suggest much in what they *do not* tell. They suggest that, like Lehi, we cannot bypass our responsibility to read, interpret, and wrestle with the word of the Lord in order to gain access to his presence, even were he to be present in person. In this sense, the absence of the golden plates suggests that, similarly, we will not prove the Book of Mormon's truthfulness by reconstructing its context or demonstrating that it can be plausibly incorporated into the sweep of secular history. The reader must confront the text itself and respond to its demands. The presence of the plates, like the presence of the Lord himself to Lehi, would not absolve our responsibility to read, interpret, and wrestle with what is written—and the absence of both the plates and the physical presence of the Lord redoubles that responsibility.

Of course, once we become aware of omissions in the text, we begin to notice them everywhere. For example, Lehi's second vision (see vv. 8–15) specifies that he saw the "one" descend from heaven and that "twelve others" followed, but these figures are never identified. Is the "one" Jesus, and are the "twelve" his original apostles? Or, as might be more appropriate to Lehi's time and place, is the "one" that same God whom Lehi sees sitting on his throne, and are the "twelve" representative of the twelve tribes? Does Nephi not know who they are? Or if he does, why does he not tell us? Is Lehi's vision proleptically Christian or thoroughly Jewish?

Or we might take an even starker example. Nephi's account of his father's second vision stretches in some detail over the span of eight verses. We are told later on, as Lehi is preaching, that the things Lehi reads in the book in his vision "manifested plainly of the coming of a Messiah and also the redemption of the world" (v. 19), but Nephi's detailed account of the vision itself never mentions a messiah at any point. Why displace this information from the vision itself? Why defer its inclusion until his summary of Lehi's preaching? Why mention it only in passing and after the fact? Similarly, why omit from his version of his father's visions any account of his father receiving a formal call as a prophet bearing the word of the Lord? Again, we are told after the fact and in passing in 1 Nephi 2:1 that Lehi was officially commissioned like Isaiah (see Isaiah 6:8–9)—but why displace this information from his account of the vision itself? Nephi appears to have purposefully omitted from his initial account of his father's visions what we might consider its two most important elements: God's promise of a messiah and Lehi's explicit commission as a prophet.

These questions need further consideration, but ultimately they suggest that selection, omission, deferral, and displacement are at the heart of scripture. Scripture is impossible without them. Revelation proceeds not just by way of addition but also by way of subtraction. In order to be revealed, something must be foregrounded. But in order to be foregrounded, that same thing must be selected and separated. And this process of selection and abridgment is also, necessarily, a process that involves omission and deferral. In order to give with one hand, God must take with the other. In order to show us one thing (for example, the Book of Mormon), God must displace another (for example, the golden plates). Nephi's omissions highlight our responsibility as readers to read carefully—and to do so with awareness of our limitations and of the text's freedom to displace our desires and expectations.

Question 4: What does it mean to be made "mighty, even unto the power of deliverance," and how is the character of this deliverance clarified by the promise of "tender mercies" (1 Nephi 1:20)? What relationship does such deliverance have to the ongoing experience of loss and affliction (see v. 1)?

Nephi interrupts his narrative of Lehi's prophetic career in Jerusalem at a critical moment. He interrupts his account of an audience angry enough to want Lehi dead to restate and clarify the aims of his theological project. Nephi's direct, second-person address is arresting: "But behold, I Nephi will shew unto you that the tender mercies of the Lord is over all them whom he hath chosen because of their faith to make them mighty, even unto the power of deliverance" (1 Nephi 1:20). While Nephi explains his approach, we wait in suspense: will Lehi be "cast out and stoned and slain" by the Jews in Jerusalem as the "prophets of old" (v. 20)? The incongruity between Nephi's confidence and Lehi's plight propels us to interpretative work. When Nephi resumes the narrative, Lehi receives another vision in which God commands him to "depart into the wilderness" (1 Nephi 2:2). Obeying this commandment averts Lehi's premature death, yet the cost is that Lehi must leave his home, land, and inheritance. Deliverance comes at a high price. And rather than involving a mighty display of power, deliverance involves Lehi sneaking quietly out of town. What is Nephi claiming here about God's "power of deliverance"?

One way of answering these questions is to consider the meaning and function of the Lord's "tender mercies" in this deliverance. The phrase *tender mercies* is not unique to the Book of Mormon. The phrase appears ten times in the psalms of the King James Bible (1611). It entered English scriptural idiom through Miles Coverdale's translation of the Bible in 1535. The English reformers employed the phrase *tender mercies* to render the Hebrew word *raḥămîm*, an intensive, plural nominal form of the verb *rāḥam* meaning "to love, have compassion." The root of the various forms and cognates of *rḥm* refers to an intense, visceral love, the love that a mother has for a child of her womb and, by extension, the love that God feels for his creation, particularly for those in covenantal relation with him. The completely dependent nature of the baby activates the mother's tender care, protective compassion, and perpetual mercy—characteristics of God's nature as revealed to Moses on Mount Sinai: "The Lord, the Lord, a God merciful [*raḥûm*] and gracious, slow to anger, and abounding in steadfast love [*ḥesed*] and faithfulness" (Exodus 34:6). The theology of grace in the Hebrew Bible is rooted in God's self-description and is articulated in Israel's praises and prayers, especially in the psalms. Israel learns through repeated suffering, captivity, and disobedience that "knowledge of God's character and the mysterious way of God's providence wins out over political expediency."[2] Although divine compassion prevails over divine judgment and transforms Israel's external circumstances, "the ultimate expression of divine compassion is the mending" of their internal dispositions.[3] In verse 20, Nephi evokes this theology of grace and offers to teach us about this divine mystery: the role of suffering affliction and exercising faith in becoming favored or chosen of God, a paradox that he introduces at the beginning of his record in verse 1.

In the first verse of 1 Nephi 1, Nephi claims to have been given "a great knowledge of the goodness and the mysteries of God." This knowledge is closely tied to his experience of "many afflictions." The structure of this verse is complex but instructive. The structure depends on the repetition of two key words: *therefore* and *having*. The word *therefore* is repeated twice and divides the verse into two parallel sections: (1) "having been born ... therefore I was taught," and (2) "having seen many afflictions ... therefore I make a record." This is straightforward, but Nephi also feels moved to clarify his experience of afflictions with the addition of two qualifications: "having seen many afflictions

---

2. Michael P. Knowles, *The Unfolding Mystery of the Divine Name: The God of Sinai in Our Midst* (Downers Grove, IL: InterVarsity Press, 2012), 68.

3. Knowles, *Unfolding Mystery of the Divine Name*, 70.

in the course of my days, nevertheless having been highly favored of the Lord in all my days, yea, having had a great knowledge of the goodness and the mysteries of God ...." His experience of affliction, although taxing, was conditioned by his simultaneous experience of God's favor. Though he was afflicted, *nevertheless* he was "highly favored."

The "mysteries of God" revealed to Nephi center on his "nevertheless." How is it possible to both suffer afflictions *and* be highly favored of the Lord? Nephi's "nevertheless" names in a single word the kind of mighty deliverance the Lord promises to send and the form that his tender mercies will take. God's mercy and deliverance will arrive in conjunction with the experiences of loss and affliction rather than as any simple freedom from these experiences. God's mercy is tender because it is both sensitive to our needs and vulnerable to life's losses and bruises. Rather than eliminating our troubles, God's power works with and through them to make sure that, whatever we suffer, his saving favor will have "never been less" as a result.

Huldah's Long Shadow

Julie M. Smith

LEHI SAW THE THRONE OF GOD IN A VISION and began preaching in 597 BCE (see 1 Nephi 1:4). About twenty-five years before that, he had witnessed a radical religious reformation in Jerusalem. It began when King Josiah ordered that the temple be renovated (see 2 Kings 22). During that process, a book[1] was discovered in the temple. Upon learning of its contents,[2] Josiah was penitent and mourned for the wickedness of his people. Desiring to know the Lord's will,[3] he consulted the prophetess Huldah. It seems very likely that Huldah and Lehi would have known each other: they lived at the same time, not only in Jerusalem but probably

---

1. This "book" was actually a scroll.

2. The text never specifies which scroll this is; scholars generally conclude that it is all or part (perhaps chapters 27–28 or 32) of the book of Deuteronomy, although likely not identical to the version that would later be canonized.

3. Many readers assume that Josiah seeks out a prophet's word in order to determine if the scroll is genuine. But this seems unlikely because Josiah immediately rends his garments when he hears the text read (2 Kings 22:11), leading to the conclusion that he accepts the validity of the text even before consulting Huldah. Thus it seems more likely that he seeks a prophetic word in response to the text in order to interpret the text or to determine what his response to the text should be. Further support for this reading comes from the fact that the response Huldah gives does not authenticate the text but rather interprets it (2 Kings 22:15–20).

1

in the same section of the city.[4] Huldah responded to King Josiah's request with two messages from the Lord: first, that disaster would come to Jerusalem as a result of their iniquity and, second, that Josiah would be spared from this destruction—but only because he would die beforehand. In response, King Josiah purged the temple of idols, initiated a covenant renewal ceremony, and reinstituted the celebration of the Passover.

I would like to explore how these events—which are recounted in 2 Kings 22 and 2 Chronicles 34—might nuance the readers' understanding of the first chapter of the Book of Mormon. My observations will stem from two distinct approaches to the text: first historical and then literary. I will then comment briefly on how Huldah's and Lehi's stories can help readers navigate the potential pitfalls of historical and literary approaches to scripture.

Historical reading

The reaction to Huldah's word from the Lord is momentous: the king organizes a ceremony where all the people in Jerusalem[5]—from the very youngest to the oldest—enter into the covenant. A complete

---

4. Huldah lived in the Mishneh or second quarter (see 2 Kings 22:14; the KJV refers, inaccurately, to the "college"); this part of Jerusalem is a later addition that was home to many who had migrated from the north, a group that likely included Lehi's family in previous generations. This conclusion is based on Alma 10:3, which locates Lehi's ancestors among the northern tribes who apparently fled into Judah to escape the Assyrian invasion. See Jeffrey R. Chadwick, "Lehi's House at Jerusalem and the Land of His Inheritance," in *Glimpses of Lehi's Jerusalem*, ed. John W. Welch, David Rolph Seely, and Jo Ann H. Seely (Provo, UT: FARMS, 2004). See also David Rolph Seely and Jo Ann H. Seely, "Lehi and Jeremiah: Prophets, Priests, and Patriarchs," *Journal of Book of Mormon Studies* 8/2 (1999): 24–35, 85–86. Huldah may also be one of the prophets mentioned in 1 Nephi 1:4. In addition, most readings of 1 Nephi 5:12–13 would lead to the conclusion that the plates contained a record of Huldah's story, so even if Lehi had somehow not been previously aware of (some elements of) it, Lehi and Nephi would have learned about it from the brass plates.

5. It is possible that this reference to "all" is hyperbole, but even if so, the scope and drama of the reforms initiated by Huldah's proclamation are such that Lehi must have been aware of them.

purging of the idols and the paraphernalia of idol worship follows, and the people once again celebrate the Passover. Lehi had lived in Jerusalem all his days up to this point (see 1 Nephi 1:4), so a historical reading assumes that Lehi participated in this covenant renewal and observed the dramatic destruction of the idols. How would these events have impacted Lehi?

First, Lehi likely expected his own preaching to be well received. After all, he had witnessed a situation very similar to his own—one where a prophetic figure received a divine book and preached about the impending destruction of Jerusalem—and the response to her was very positive. He had good reason to believe that his preaching would be met, as was Huldah's, with repentance and recommitment.[6] If anything, he might have suspected that his book, straight from heaven, would yield better results than Huldah's. So his audience's mockery might have come as a shock to him. Perhaps some derided him because they assumed that the necessary reforms had already taken place.[7] This is the very argument that Nephi's brothers later made against Lehi (see 1 Nephi 17:22). It is also possible that otherwise righteous people—including, perhaps, some of his own sons—rejected Lehi's message because they assumed that their supposed individual righteousness would protect them, as it had Josiah, from experiencing the consequences of other people's wickedness. Perhaps others assumed that if twenty-five years had passed with no clear fulfillment of Huldah's prophecy of destruction, there was no point in continuing to worry about it. Maybe Lehi's audience contrasted him unfavorably with Huldah, who, after all, had an actual, physical book that others could touch, see, and read and not just something that she claimed to have seen in a dream. Perhaps some of Laman and Lemuel's difficulty with accepting their father's preaching stemmed from a belief that true prophets garner a response more akin to Huldah's than Lehi's. It seems

---

6. While other prophets received a negative response to their preaching, the fact that Lehi shared with Huldah access to a sacred book probably makes her the best model for his expectations.

7. Despite all the iniquity described in the Book of Mormon, the book makes very litte reference to idolatry. Possibly the recent round of reforms under Huldah, which included a purging of the paraphernalia of idolatry, led to this state of affairs.

likely that Lehi's initial optimism would have been quashed by the response to his preaching, which would presumably have been very painful for him; perhaps he even doubted his own commission (which is not specifically included in the text, unlike in other similar prophetic call stories)[8] and wondered if he had somehow misunderstood or failed. Immediately after relating that Lehi's life was threatened by his preaching, Nephi announces his intention to show readers the tender mercies of the Lord and then recounts that the Lord spoke to Lehi, reassuring him that he had been faithful and was blessed for what he had done. The Lord specifically indicates that it is precisely because of Lehi's faithfulness that the people are trying to kill him.[9] This passage may be best understood in the context of Lehi's surprise at the negative response to his preaching.

Second, most readers of the Book of Mormon probably presume that Lehi's book[10] contains a record of the abominations of the people, thus leading to his pronouncement of woes. However, a comparison with Huldah's story might lead to a different conclusion. In Huldah's situation, there is general agreement that the book is (some version of) the book of Deuteronomy. But Deuteronomy does not contain a listing of abominations in Huldah's day. Instead, it is a list of laws: King Josiah does not mourn because he has read a register of the people's sins but rather because it is now apparent to him that the people are not following the law. While certainty is not possible, the similarities between Huldah's and Lehi's experiences suggest that Lehi, too, may have been given in his vision a book containing a law code and that it is his reading of the law that leads him to pronounce woes upon

---

8. See Blake Thomas Ostler, "The Throne-Theophany and Prophetic Commission in 1 Nephi: A Form-Critical Analysis," *BYU Studies* 26/4 (1986): 67–95.

9. The current chapter divisions in the Book of Mormon are not original to the text. The original chapter divisions (which apparently represent divisions indicated on the plates) take all of 1 Nephi 1–5 as one chapter. So it may make more sense to consider 1 Nephi 2:1 as the final line of 1 Nephi 1; doing this would emphasize Lehi's faithfulness despite the unfortunate and unexpected response to his call.

10. It is interesting to speculate about the nature of Lehi's book: Was it an old book—taken to heaven, preserved, and then returned to earth, as if resurrected? Was it a future book, perhaps even the Book of Mormon itself?

Jerusalem. This interpretation helps explain an otherwise perplexing feature of Lehi's response to reading the book: he announces, "great and marvelous are thy works, O Lord God Almighty ... because thou art merciful, thou wilt not suffer those who come unto thee that they shall perish" (1 Nephi 1:14). This is a rather odd response to a book that listed sins and promised destruction, but it is a sensible response to a book containing a law code—a code that shows a way for people to "come unto [God]" by observing the law.

Third, Nephi seems particularly concerned about his writing. In a manner unparalleled elsewhere,[11] he signals that he is deeply anxious to establish the validity of his record. He notes that he wrote it himself, that he knows it is true, that he made the record with his own hand, and that he condensed his father's writings. He also speaks directly to his audience to emphasize his desire that they will know Lehi's story. This anxiety may stem from the impact that Huldah's experience had on Lehi and that Lehi in turn transmitted to Nephi.[12] Although the initial response to Huldah's word from the Lord was overwhelmingly positive, in the longer term, the reaction was more complex. When, as Huldah had prophesied, calamity was poured out on the inhabitants of Jerusalem in the form of an attack from Babylon, there was debate as to whether it was, as Huldah had taught, the result of the people's wicked idolatry or whether God was punishing the people for getting rid of their idols.[13] These competing explanations, which could have stemmed

---

11. There is some resonance with Deuteronomy 4:2; John 20:30–31; and Revelation 22:18–19, but Nephi's depth of concern for his record is unmatched in the Bible.

12. Nephi hints at this in 1 Nephi 1:1. Precise dates are unknowable, but it is likely that Lehi would have been a young man at the time of Josiah's reforms. It is even possible that a very young Laman and Lemuel witnessed the dramatic destruction of the idols; if this was the case, this formative experience may explain some of the gap in attitude between Laman and Lemuel on the one hand and Nephi and Sam on the other.

13. See Jeremiah 44:15–18. Interestingly, this viewpoint—quoted disapprovingly in Jeremiah—has been making a comeback among Latter-day Saints under the influence of Margaret Barker, who argues that Josiah's reforms negated earlier, more correct worship practices. There are solid reasons to dispute Barker's thesis, not the least of which is that it requires taking the position that a vast portion of the Hebrew Bible advocates false religion. At the same time, it is worth noting that one of the items specifically mentioned as being destroyed in Josiah's purging of idols is a tree that symbolized the divine

from the murky origin of the book found in the temple, may have led to Nephi's intense need to assure his audience of the authenticity of his own record. Further support for this reading comes from the contrast between the role of the scribes as intermediaries in Huldah's story and Nephi's repeated emphasis that he, on the other hand, made his record with his own hand (1 Nephi 1:3 and 17).

Next, commenters have long noted the absence of women's stories and women's voices from the Book of Mormon. This is in stark contrast to Huldah's story, where perhaps what is most remarkable about her gender is that it is not mentioned, despite the fact that the high priest assigned a woman the task of receiving and transmitting the word of God to the king in a situation where male prophets were active and where it was of crucial importance that the prophetic utterance be indisputable.[14] Since this is the context of Lehi's life in Jerusalem, why, then, is the situation in the Book of Mormon so different? I should note first that women are more prominent in Nephi's narrative than in the rest of the Book of Mormon.[15] So I might hypothesize that the

feminine (see 2 Kings 23:6; the KJV is not clear here, but a representation of Asherah is destroyed), but in Nephi's vision, he sees a tree and is taught that it symbolizes the mother of the son of God (see 1 Nephi 11:8–13). See also Daniel C. Peterson, "Nephi and His Asherah," *Journal of Book of Mormon Studies* 9/2 (2000): 16–25 and 80–81. So it may be that Josiah's reforms were fundamentally sound but slightly excessive, and Lehi's experience offers a recorrection of Josiah's overcorrection. While speculative, it is possible that the prophets in 1 Nephi 1:4 are arguing that the people need to "repent" for abandoning their idol worship and, further, that Lehi's confusion over which voices are correct leads to his prayer (in a situation remarkably similar to what led to Joseph Smith's first vision).

14. Huldah's high status is further emphasized by the fact that the delegation from the king travels to her and not vice versa (see 2 Kings 22:14). Also, she repeatedly uses the phrase "thus saith the Lord" (2 Kings 22:15, 16, and 18). Note that her status as a prophet must have been well established before this incident; otherwise, the high priest would not have chosen her for this assignment.

15. The role of women is especially prominent in what was originally the first chapter of the Book of Mormon (now 1 Nephi 1–5). The quick shift from "goodly parents" in 1 Nephi 1:1 to "father" sets up the expectation that Nephi will return to the issue of his mother, which he does in 1 Nephi 5. This original first chapter was bookended by the stories of how Lehi and Sariah became convinced of his calling. The text shows Sariah gaining her own, independent knowledge (see 1 Nephi 5:8) of her husband's

absence of women stems from later redaction of the Book of Mormon instead of the experiences of Lehi's family. Another possibility is that the later lack of female voices reflects the increasing wickedness of the society: if Lehi experienced a prime prophetic voice as female and if this expectation were transmitted through the generations, then one way for the narrative to signal decline would be for society to silence female voices.[16] (Interestingly, the Lamanites seemingly have a keener sensitivity to women's concerns than the Nephites do.)[17]

Fifth, Huldah's experience accentuates the importance of the written record: without it, the people had grievously strayed, and when they reencounter the law, they are confronted with a chasm between it and their own behavior, a tragic gap that they had not realized before encountering the text. They had active priests, scribes, and prophets, but this was not enough to ensure fidelity in the absence of a written text. This same concern for the written word—a concern that may be

---

commission, and her experience, along with Lehi's, frames the first chapter of the text. (If the family was intimately familiar with Huldah's story, it is even possible that 1 Nephi 5 is modeled on Huldah's experience, with Sariah in effect reenacting the experience.) In fact, a particular theme of 1 Nephi 5 is Lehi's inability to convince Sariah. His words may have provided comfort to Sariah, but they could not provide knowledge or joy—only her personal experience could do that (see 1 Nephi 5:6–8). Further, several structural elements suggest that Nephi intended the reader to compare Lehi's experience in 1 Nephi 1 with Sariah's in 1 Nephi 5: (1) for both, a return trip to Jerusalem was needed in order that revelation could be received; (2) each revelatory experience is immediately followed by Lehi's studying a new sacred record; (3) a main concern in both situations is "preserving the commandments" (see 1 Nephi 5:21); (4) Lehi's concern with the destruction of Jerusalem parallels Sariah's concern with the destruction of her sons; and (5) they each glimpse God's mercy in response. (It may also be productive to compare Huldah with Sariah: for both, something presumably lost forever [the text, the sons] is returned, permitting a woman's voice to speak her knowledge. Also, covenant renewal and worship are the immediate result of the speech.)

16. The extraordinary events of Alma 19 as a positive climactic moment in the Book of Mormon narrative may be exemplified by the role that Abish plays in voicing God's role in events (see Alma 19:17). Like Huldah, Abish is one who serves as a messenger to show that a dead text/body is not truly dead but merely requires a spiritually attuned messenger to bring it back to life.

17. See Grant Hardy, *Understanding the Book of Mormon: A Reader's Guide* (New York: Oxford University Press, 2010), 46–47.

directly based on Lehi's memory of Huldah's reforms—permeates the Book of Mormon, where even the most casual reader quickly becomes aware of the repeated emphasis on the necessity of written records (see, for example, Mosiah 1:4). When Nephi, mentally girding himself to kill Laban, thinks that "they could not keep the commandments of the Lord according to the law of Moses save they should have the law" (1 Nephi 4:15), he may very well be recalling what Lehi has taught him about the lessons of Huldah's reforms.[18]

Literary reading

Now I shift my gaze away from strictly historical matters and toward a literary reading. Here I am less concerned with the historical context of events and instead consider Huldah's and Lehi's stories as if they were two case studies that can by analyzed in order to reflect upon their shared themes and patterns.

    Huldah and Lehi are each given a book. Huldah's is recovered only because Josiah showed interest in restoring the temple. While not explicitly stated, readers can speculate that the text she received had been deliberately prepared to be read by those—and only by those—who would refurbish the temple. One might even say that it was hidden up for that purpose. Similarly, Lehi's prayers led to his experience with the pillar of fire, which led to his exhaustion on his bed, which led to his vision of the book. On both occasions, the book was awaiting the ones who sought out a closer connection to the divine, and the prophet is asked to read the book: Huldah is asked by King Josiah and Lehi is asked by the One associated with the throne of God. Each time, the person[19] who requests the reading is already familiar with the contents of the book. They request the reading not because the text itself will

---

    18. Because the temple restoration begins by using the silver that had been donated to the temple for repairs (see 2 Kings 22:4–5), there is a sense in which money has been traded for the book found in the temple. Similarly, in the Book of Mormon narrative, Nephi's attempt to trade silver (and gold) for Laban's record may echo what he has learned of Josiah's experience.

    19. The text of 1 Nephi 1 does not clarify whether the "one" who descends is the person who was sitting on the throne (in which case the parallel to King Josiah is very

provide them with new information but rather because the text creates an opportunity for a prophetic response. This idea might nuance our understanding of the purpose of reading: it is not limited to conveying information but also serves as a springboard to new revelation. If they define the term *translation* broadly, then readers can consider both Huldah and Lehi as translating the texts that they read, in the sense of using them as source material from which to proclaim the word of the Lord anew. This paradigm might be a useful one for thinking about some of Joseph Smith's translation work, particularly his translation of the Bible and the Book of Abraham.

It is easy to imagine Huldah's book gathering dust in a neglected, hidden corner in the temple,[20] while Lehi's book, newly descended from heaven, would presumably be pristine. And yet Huldah's book can be touched and read by anyone while Lehi's exists only in his vision and is therefore inaccessible to anyone else. Consequently, recourse to a book seen only in a vision may be one of the worst ways to convince a hostile audience of the genuine nature of the prophetic message. So in both instances, the book's pedigree is compromised—but in different ways. I will return later to the implications of the imperfect nature of each text, but for now I will simply note that a divine book is not a perfect book—or a perfectly pedigreed book, or a perfectly accessible book.

Neither the reader of 2 Kings nor the reader of 1 Nephi is given the content of the book. This lacuna emphasizes the response each prophet has to the book; what Huldah's reader and Lehi's reader experience is not the book itself but rather the prophetic response to the book. In other words, the book is not important per se since the prophetic "translation" is accentuated. Huldah and Lehi each respond to the text with a similar prophetic utterance in two parts. The first halves closely track each other since they concern the impending destruction

---

tight) or is the deputy of the person who sits on the throne (in which case it is still substantial, if not as tight).

20. The account in 2 Kings does not specify where the text was found, but if it came from the holy of holies—which was understood to represent the Lord's seat or throne—then the comparison with Lehi's account is even tighter.

of Jerusalem for its wickedness.[21] Neither prophecy is conditional; the coming destruction is announced but not the possibility of avoiding it through repentance. It seems that for both Huldah's and Lehi's audiences, the time has come when it is "everlastingly too late" to repent (Helaman 13:38).[22] This state of affairs raises some interesting questions about the purpose of the text and the prophetic response to the text: What is the point of a new text and a prophetic utterance if repentance is not possible? Readers might assume that in Lehi's situation, the purpose was to get his family out of Jerusalem to avoid the coming destruction, but that command will come from an entirely separate dream in 1 Nephi 2:1–2. So both Huldah and Lehi announce destruction that cannot be avoided for (and, later, mercy that does not apply to) most of their audience. Why? This question asks us to rethink the point of prophecy. In these instances, it is clearly not for the immediate benefit of the audience but perhaps for future audiences to see how the prophecy was in fact fulfilled. In this way, the prophetic voice is capable of rupturing time—it speaks not to its own generation, not for its own benefit, but to a future reader. This situation ties in nicely with the move that Nephi will soon make in 1 Nephi 1:18 and 20 of speaking directly to his future readers. That, too, is an act of the prophetic voice.

Surprisingly enough, mercy is the second theme in both accounts: Huldah announces mercy for Josiah, and Lehi proclaims the Lord's mercy. Additionally, both accounts tie mercy to monarchy: Huldah refers specifically to the king while Lehi's words make reference to the throne of God and thus emphasize God's kingly elements. The antimonarchist rhetoric in many parts of the Hebrew Bible is strong; the minimization of this theme in the Book of Mormon and the very positive portrayal of, for example, King Benjamin, might be indirectly

---

21. Huldah says that the Lord will bring evil upon "this place" (2 Kings 22:16), which can be understood as Jerusalem or as all of Judah. In 2 Kings 23:27, the word of the Lord comes through an unnamed prophet (likely Huldah, given that she appears to be the king's choice of prophets to deliver new oracles) and announces the destruction of Judah and Jerusalem.

22. While speculative, it is possible that this predicament explains the "missing commission" in Lehi's prophetic call narrative: he is not commissioned because he does not, like other prophets (compare Isaiah 6:9–11), preach repentance.

attributable to the theme of monarchical mercy found in Huldah's and Lehi's statements.

The juxtaposition of destruction and mercy is as startling as it is comforting. This odd duo highlights the need for a prophetic voice in response to a text: that voice frames and nuances the message in what is essentially an act of translation. Both interpreted texts mitigate the stereotypical view of the retributive, punishing God by balancing the message of destruction for wickedness with the promise of God's mercy. The prophetic message to Josiah is the same as the one to Lehi:[23] because of his righteousness, he will be spared the need to witness the destruction of Jerusalem. In both cases, the admixture of judgment and mercy relies on the idea of a *place* being judged but of an *individual* being spared. The rupture between location and inhabitant sets the stage for Lehi's journey out of Jerusalem. And further complicating the message of mercy is the fact that both Josiah's and Lehi's silver lining accompanies a very dark cloud indeed: the only reason Josiah will be spared the destruction is that he will die before it happens. Similarly, Lehi's statement that God will "not suffer those who come unto [him] that they shall perish" (1 Nephi 1:14) weighs differently under the burden of knowing that his family will come very close to perishing[24] and will lose their community, wealth, and family unity. Personal righteousness is enough to prevent some level of harm, but not all of it. Maybe not even most of it. The individual can be disentangled from the community to an extent (and thus moral agency is preserved), but not entirely, and thus Josiah and Lehi escape the destruction of Jerusalem only by the most painful of means.[25] The prophetic responses

---

23. This link may be strengthened by Huldah's announcement that Josiah will be shown mercy because his heart was "tender" (see 2 Kings 22:19) and by Nephi's thesis at the end of the chapter that the Lord's "tender" mercies (see 1 Nephi 1:20) are over the faithful.

24. See 1 Nephi 2:11; 5:2; 16:39; 17:5; 19:20.

25. Given that Josiah dies in battle, the idea of his going to his grave "in peace" (see 2 Kings 22:20) is somewhat difficult to understand. Possibilities include that (1) he had a peaceful and honorable burial in Judah; (2) he did not in fact have a peaceful death because he violated prophetic counsel and returned to battle (see 2 Chronicles 35:20–22); (3) had he obeyed, things might have played out differently; and (4) he will be at peace

ɔth Huldah and Lehi share an identical message concerning the complicated relationship between destruction and mercy.

Huldah and Lehi: Historical and literary approaches

Now that I have explored the outlines of a historical and a literary reading of the relationship between Huldah and Lehi, it is time to complicate the picture by considering the limitations of these readings. Obviously, if Lehi was one of the people present at King Josiah's covenant renewal ceremony, it only makes sense to consider how this event would have shaped the background to 1 Nephi 1; it would be foolish to ignore an avenue that could potentially provide new insights into the Book of Mormon narrative. At the same time, reading historically is problematic. In this situation, Huldah's story is recounted in two canonized texts;[26] comparing these two accounts makes clear that at least one—if not both—of their authors has molded a historical narrative in order to advance distinct theological interests.[27] This is most obvious in 2 Kings' focus on the destruction of the idols when contrasted with 2 Chronicles' attention to the reinstitution of the Passover. However, other differences as well, including the fact that the texts do not share the same order of events, raise questions about causality. Further, many scholars wonder whether the ancient book discovered in the temple still had wet ink—that is, whether it was a recent creation designed to legitimize reforms that Josiah already desired to implement. The reader is left with irreconcilable accounts and no reliable, solid way to determine what actually happened. How, then, could this precarious account clarify Lehi's situation? The impenetrability of this question

---

after death because of his righteousness. It may be that the promise of going to his grave in peace actually hints at a violent death, since those are the likely circumstances under which a decent burial is an open question.

26. See 2 Kings 22 and 2 Chronicles 34.

27. This paper follows the account in 2 Kings 22, which emphasizes the purge of the idols, because it is generally regarded as the earlier text. The account in 2 Chronicles 34 is far more focused on the reinstitution of the Passover and merits further study alongside Lehi's experience given that his family will, in effect, enact a new exodus.

might lead readers to favor literary readings, but those are equally—if differently—fraught. What surety can there be as to whether any particular literary observation is inherent to the text or the product of the interpreter's own imposition? A second trouble that readers face when attempting a literary reading of the Book of Mormon is the inability to determine whether a particular word, phrase, or structure originated with its author, with the editor, or with Joseph Smith. So while Lehi's audience might have missed the mark by questioning his vision of the interpretation of books, the modern reader would probably bat well above average by adopting the same posture when presented with an interpretation. But if we delegitimate both historical and literary readings, what is left? How, then, might we interpret the text?

This is a swift rapid in a narrow shoal, but one that Huldah and Lehi can help readers navigate. Each audience has reason to doubt its text and its interpretation of it: in Huldah's case, because the author and origin of the text is completely unknown, and in Lehi's, because the text exists only in his vision and is not accessible to the audience. But both times the audience does not need to rely solely on the witness of the text, as it is combined with the authoritative word of the prophet. Further, in each situation, the audience is empowered to reach its own conclusions about the text: just as Josiah reads and rends his clothes, Nephi directly addresses his audience and invites them to know for themselves concerning what he is writing.[28] The brilliance of both Huldah's and Lehi's experiences is the way in which each story holds in tight tension the various avenues of revelation in order to convey to the audience that revelation does not depend upon a single slender thread but is instead an interwoven tapestry. For Huldah, revelation occurs because the king initiates temple repairs, because the high priest finds the scroll, because the scribes read the scroll, and because the prophetess Huldah receives the word of the Lord regarding the scroll. There is a balance here. Nephi presents a similar balance: attestations

---

28. Nephi's direct references to the audience via second-person pronouns (see 1 Nephi 1:18 and 20) nicely mirrors the other use of this rare narrative technique in Moroni 10.

of the validity of his record, the careful use of sources,[29] the vision, the dream, and the book are the different stakes pinning down the revealed will. Lehi's situation is particularly striking in that a divine being asks him to read a book. One might presume that that person could have directly communicated to Lehi whatever it was that needed to be said; a book is formally unnecessary in a face-to-face setting.[30] So Lehi's experience emphasizes the importance of the book and its mediating role—even in the very presence of one just descended from heaven. Similarly, one can imagine Huldah announcing the word of the Lord without a newly discovered book. The book is, again, formally unnecessary so that its presence emphasizes the mediating role of texts, even for an authoritative and well-respected prophet. For both Lehi and Huldah, revelation does not come through one channel but is reinforced, clarified, and interpreted through different venues. Even a book straight from the temple or from heaven requires interpretation.[31] The Book of Mormon continues this theme by showing that even Lehi's wife did not believe in his calling until she had her own witness of it; similarly, Nephi asks to see what his father saw to gain an independent witness of it (1 Nephi 11:1).

In both Lehi's and Huldah's stories, it is clear that the Spirit is operative in their ability to read the text: in Lehi's case, because Nephi specifies that he was filled with the Spirit as he read (see 1 Nephi 1:12),

---

29. In 1 Nephi 1:16–17, Nephi makes clear that he will abridge his father's record, but he will make a fuller account of his own days. Lehi's record reflects Lehi's—not Nephi's—own knowledge, and so of course Nephi's account of it will of necessity be incomplete. Nephi will not be providing a full account of his father's experiences. He cannot; it is not his own experience. Nephi is very careful to draw a distinction between records where he is the primary source—material that he will relate in full and to which he can assent to its truthfulness—versus material that he abridges and that draws from experiences not his own. Surprisingly, Nephi does not class his father's records as beyond reproach, but he rather carefully delineates a difference between them and his own.

30. Similarly, one wonders why the plates were necessary for Joseph Smith to translate, given that he apparently sometimes translated without looking at the plates. It seems that the necessity for the text is something other than strictly functional.

31. Similarly, later Lehi and Nephi will see (what is apparently) the same vision, but they offer radically different interpretations of it.

and in Huldah's, because her triple repetition of the phrase "thus saith the Lord"[32] implies that the Lord's Spirit is within her and prompts her speech. So the Spirit is yet another check on the process.

Lehi's and Huldah's stories simultaneously emphasize and de-emphasize the importance of texts by, on the one hand, making the text central to the development of the narrative—even when it is not formally necessary—and, on the other hand, including a variety of mediators of the text. Each time the role of the prophet as interpreter and translator of the text is emphasized. The role of a book is, as Isaiah wrote and as Nephi quoted, to make it possible that "the words of the faithful should speak as if it were from the dead" (2 Nephi 27:13). In other words, when a prophet interprets a text, the prophet has resurrected the text.

For both Josiah and Lehi, the mercy they receive is predicated not on the book per se but rather on the prophetic response to the book. And while one can easily imagine both Huldah's and Lehi's stories proceeding with no book at all—simply with divine revelation coming to the prophet without the mediating text—the presence of the text speaks to its important mediating role. With Huldah, the presence of prophets was incapable of maintaining righteousness in the absence of the written word, but the written word was incapable of being fully understood and implemented without her prophetic interpretation of it. The book can be an aid to memory, a way to displace time, and a prompt to new prophetic inspiration. But it is not an end in itself. The same dynamic might apply to the work of Joseph Smith, where, for example, his work on the Joseph Smith Translation of the Bible led to many revelations for what would later become the Doctrine and Covenants. The message to the reader is clear: as important as a text is in understanding the will of God, it is but one step in a process that consists of, in a more modern analogy, a variety of checks and balances. The problems of the text—whether the provenance of Huldah's, the reality of Lehi's, or the stumbling blocks hiding in a historical or literary reading—are solved not by proving anything outright but rather by balancing a slew of methods and modes of revelation. Thus, the book

---

32. See 2 Kings 22:15, 16, and 18.

is never an end in itself; the book is a link in the chain of revelation. Huldah and Lehi are two witnesses to the same pattern: they are each given a book of sacred origin, and their response to reading the text is to prophesy. They have thus taught readers how to account for the fact that it is impossible to prove the provenance—or the literary nature—of the text. They translate their texts—not into another tongue but rather into another tone—to show that while texts always mediate the divine presence, prophets always mediate the text.[33]

Conclusions

Given the historical proximity to and importance of Huldah's experience to Lehi's life, and given the myriad ways in which Lehi's story echoes and amplifies Huldah's, readers have good reason to argue that Huldah casts a shadow over the entire Book of Mormon narrative, but especially the first chapter. Her concern with texts is unlike anything seen elsewhere in the Bible yet is perfectly at home with the near obsession with texts, records, and the prophetic responses to them that permeates the Book of Mormon. Her prophecy emphasizes commandments and mercy, which will become two key themes in the Book of Mormon. It is also pinned to history by its prophecy of the destruction of Jerusalem, which is the signal event in the inauguration of the Book of Mormon narrative. She is the mother of the "likening it unto yourself" hermeneutic that is so very characteristic of the Book of Mormon. And if one goal of the Book of Mormon is to convince the reader that new revelation is possible, there are few better ways to do that than by reference to Huldah's experience. The pattern is simple: receive a divine book, read the book, and engage the book with your world through the prophetic voice. Huldah sets a pattern followed by Lehi, by Alma,[34] by Joseph Smith, and, ideally, by every modern reader of the Book of Mormon.

---

33. Contrast Matthew 2:4–6, where the chief priests and scribes can recite the text but cannot apply it to their current circumstance.

34. See Joseph M. Spencer, *An Other Testament: On Typology*, 2nd ed. (Provo, UT: Neal A. Maxwell Institute for Religious Scholarship, 2016), 8–9.

Burnt Offerings: Favor, Afflictions, and the Mysteries of God

Adam S. Miller

Lehi in the desert

WHERE IS LEHI GOING? What is he aiming to do? And, then, when the fire comes, what does he see and what does he hear?

We have only a handful of sentences. We know only the few details Nephi chooses to tell. And, to be fair, Nephi is trying to tell the story of his own life, not his father's—though, like all of us, he can only tell his story by abridging his father's life into his own. So, when the narration begins in the first chapter of 1 Nephi, Nephi begins with his father's story. On Nephi's account, his father's story starts midway through life when Lehi is already a grown man, already a father with children who are themselves almost grown. His story starts "in the commencement of the first year of the reign of Zedekiah, king of Judah" (1 Nephi 1:4). This is useful information, but Nephi is not especially interested in kings. He's just setting the stage. Rather, he's interested in how "in that same year there came many prophets prophesying unto the people that they must repent or the great city Jerusalem must be destroyed" (1 Nephi 1:4).

Lehi gets moving in response to these prophets. Their words seem to shake loose some previously fixed part of him. So Lehi goes out. "Wherefore it came to pass that my father Lehi, as he went forth, prayed

17

unto the Lord, yea, even with all his heart, in behalf of his people" (1 Nephi 1:5). As he will frequently do in the verses that follow (cf. 1 Nephi 1:5, 6, 12, 14), Nephi's narration layers his father's actions one on top of another. He narrates two things as happening at the same time: *as* Lehi is going forth, Nephi says, he is *also* praying. In this verse, the layering of action conveys a sense of urgency. It gives the impression that there's no time for Lehi to stop and pray. Even while he is going forth, he is already praying.

Where is Lehi going in such a hurry? Nephi does not say. But we can make a fair guess.

On Nephi's account, Lehi's "going forth" is explicitly linked to his hearing the call to repent. "There came many prophets prophesying unto the people that they must repent," Nephi says, "*wherefore* ... my father Lehi, as he went forth, prayed." This *wherefore* implies a direct connection between Lehi's hearing the call to repent and his going forth. And more, by way of additional confirmation, we're told that as he's going forth Lehi is already pleading on behalf of his people. Lehi, it seems safe to say, is going out to pray and repent. He's going somewhere to plead for forgiveness. And for Lehi, the ritual procedure for doing so would be clear. The protocol for his time and place is that, in order to repent, he needs to offer sacrifice. Lehi needs to make a burnt offering.

In Hebrew, the technical term for a burnt offering is *korban olah* (literally, "an offering that goes up [in smoke]"). Such sin offerings are made by slaughtering an animal (a bull, a ram, a goat, turtle doves, or pigeons), sprinkling its blood on the altar, and then burning the flesh on an altar of unhewn stones until only ashes remain. In order to offer this sacrifice, standard procedure—especially after Josiah's centralizing reforms—would have sent Lehi to the temple in Jerusalem, where priests and professionals could officiate on his behalf. But, for whatever reason, it appears that Lehi is headed *away* from Jerusalem because Nephi will later describe Lehi as having "*returned* to his own house at Jerusalem" after his first vision (1 Nephi 1:7). We also know that once Lehi leaves Jerusalem with his family in chapter 2, he won't hesitate to offer sacrifices outside the purview of the official temple cult: "And it came to pass that when he had traveled three days in the wilderness, he pitched his tent in a valley beside a river of water. And it came to pass that he built an altar of stones, and he made an offering unto the Lord and gave thanks unto the Lord our God" (1 Nephi 2:6–7). Lehi appears comfortable building his own altar and officiating in his own rituals.

But if Lehi is not going up to the temple to offer sacrifice, then where is he going? My thesis is that Lehi is headed into the desert. I suggest that, like the prophets before him and even like Jesus after him, Lehi heard the voice of the Lord, and then, having heard it, "immediately the Spirit driveth him into the wilderness" (Mark 1:12). And now, having gone off into the desert, Lehi, I think, aims to offer sacrifice. I think he means to build a stone altar and make a burnt offering. If this is right, then how far into the desert does Lehi go? And how long is he out there? A day? Three days? Forty?

The Judean desert is harsh and empty. It slopes away to the east of Jerusalem and ends with steep cliffs that border the Dead Sea. The ground between is broken and mountainous. It is full of chalky hills and terraced plateaus cut by deep, wandering ravines. Now imagine Lehi deep in these rolling, bone-dry hills, alone for days, piling up stones for an altar. Imagine Lehi slaughtering a ram, flaying its skin, up to his elbows in gore, sprinkling its blood around the edges of the altar. Imagine him praying with desperate grief on behalf of his people, praying until, as Nephi recounts it, "there came a pillar of fire and dwelt upon a rock before him, and he saw and heard much. And because of the things which he saw and heard, he did quake and tremble exceedingly" (1 Nephi 1:6). Once the vision arrives, its opening is dramatic enough that it leaves Lehi quaking, trembling, and exhausted.

But the vision's *form* probably should not come as a surprise: Lehi sees a pillar of fire. And if Lehi is deep in the desert burning a sacrifice on an altar of piled stones, then the appearance of a pillar of fire on a rock is a good fit.[1] More, it's a good fit with precedent. Whether the pillar of fire is an extension of a fire that Lehi himself sets burning or whether it falls from heaven in dramatic fashion, the result is the same: God's presence is manifest.

There are four recorded occasions in the Old Testament when a pillar of fire falls from heaven to consume a sacrifice right on the altar.

---

1. I'm indebted to Joseph Spencer for making this connection explicit.

1. God sends fire for Moses and Aaron in Leviticus 9:23–24: "And Moses and Aaron went into the tabernacle of the congregation, and came out, and blessed the people: and the glory of the Lord appeared unto all the people. And there came a fire out from before the Lord, and consumed upon the altar the burnt offering and the fat."

2. Fire falls from heaven for Solomon in 2 Chronicles 7:1–2: "Now when Solomon had made an end of praying, the fire came down from heaven, and consumed the burnt offering and the sacrifices; and the glory of the Lord filled the house. And the priests could not enter into the house of the Lord, because the glory of the Lord had filled the Lord's house."

3. Heavenly fire intervenes for Samson's father and mother in Judges 13:19–20: "So Manoah took a kid with a meat offering, and offered it upon a rock unto the Lord: and the angel did wondrously; and Manoah and his wife looked on. For it came to pass, when the flame went up toward heaven from off the altar, that the angel of the Lord ascended in the flame of the altar."

4. And, most famously, fire falls from heaven for Elijah at the climax of his duel with the priests of Baal in 1 Kings 18:37–39: "Hear me, O Lord, hear me, that this people may know that thou art the Lord God, and that thou hast turned their heart back again. Then the fire of the Lord fell, and consumed the burnt sacrifice, and the wood, and the stones, and the dust, and licked up the water that was in the trench. And when all the people saw it, they fell on their faces: and they said, The Lord, he is the God; the Lord, he is the God."

In each of these four cases, the consuming fire indicates God's acceptance of the sacrifice, and it makes his presence manifest. We should remember too that Moses, of course, hears the Lord speak to him out of a burning bush and, even more to the point, that a pillar of fire travels with Moses and the Israelites as they wander in the wilderness. Out in the desert, "the Lord went before them by day in a pillar of a cloud, to lead them the way; and by night in a pillar of fire, to give them light" (Exodus 13:21).

Once Lehi's pillar of fire arrives, Nephi tells us that his father "saw and heard much" and that "because of the things which he saw and heard, he did quake and tremble exceedingly" (1 Nephi 1:6). What, then, does Lehi see and hear? We do not know. Nephi reports only Lehi's response: seeing and hearing, Lehi quakes and trembles. And, more, he's overcome by what he sees and hears. "And it came to pass that he returned to his own house at Jerusalem. And he cast himself upon his bed, being overcome with the Spirit and the things which he had seen" (1 Nephi 1:7). Lehi is spent and, thus spent, he reaches a critical threshold. In this sense, this first of Lehi's two consecutive visions in 1 Nephi 1 feels preparatory. It harrows the ground of Lehi's soul. It readies his heart and mind for the planting of the word. In stark contrast to the detail, definition, and articulation of Lehi's second vision (1 Nephi 1:8–15), this first vision is raw and inarticulate. Where the second vision is rich with symbols, thrones, heavenly choirs, divine messengers, shouts of praise, and prophetic books, this first vision feels primal and elemental. Here there's nothing but blood and stone and fire.

Now again we are not told what Lehi see or hears, but the upshot seems clear. This first consuming vision hints darkly at the oracle of destruction ("woe unto Jerusalem") that will be clearly pronounced in the second. Staring into that fire, watching it consume his offering, Lehi would have felt in his bones the truth of what would later be articulated in the vision that follows: God will demand that he sacrifice everything because everything (like his burnt offering) is going to be consumed by fire falling from heaven. This fire may fall dramatically in a flash of lightning, or it may devour all that he loves and lives for with the slow (but inevitable) burn of time—but either way he must sacrifice everything. Lehi has no choice. He must return everything to the Lord. He must give it all up, and he must give it all back. For Lehi (as for all of us), the world as he knows it is going to end. Jerusalem is going to be destroyed.

Remember, in this connection, that there is one *other* relevant case of fire falling from heaven that we have yet to mention. And this last case involves the destruction of Sodom and Gomorrah.

Then the Lord rained upon Sodom and upon Gomorrah brimstone and fire from the Lord out of heaven; And he overthrew those cities, and all the plain, and all the inhabitants of the cities, and that which grew upon the ground.... And Abraham gat up early in the morning to the place where he stood before the Lord: and he looked toward Sodom and Gomorrah, and toward all the land of the plain, and beheld, and, lo, the smoke of the country went up as the smoke of a furnace. (Genesis 19:24–25, 27–28)

Lehi's visions are an apocalypse. He sees the end of the world and, too, he sees that the world's conflagration is both already underway and unavoidable. This world is passing away.

There is no avoiding it. *Either* (1) fire will fall from heaven to consume your sacrifice and manifest God's presence, *or* (2) fire will rain down from heaven to leave your city a smoking ruin. But have no doubt—everything will be consumed either way. As a result, Lehi has only two choices. He can either *willingly* sacrifice his home, his people, his wealth, and his land, or he can cling to them and see them destroyed. The only question here is whether the world's consumption unfolds as a sacrifice or as a judgment. Will the pillar of fire be met with shouts of praise, a gesture of consecration, and an open hand? Or will it be met with fear, regret, and a closed fist?

In telling his father's story, Nephi means to demonstrate that the Lord can make those he has chosen "mighty, even unto the power of deliverance," and that his "tender mercies" are present and palpable for those faithful to him. But along the way Nephi also plainly demonstrates that the *kind* of deliverance God offers will consistently frustrate our expectations. Often the promised deliverance works crosswise to our experience of loss and suffering, and in the main, it is a deliverance that comes to us *in* our afflictions rather than *from* them.

Lehi pleads with God in behalf of his people, and God hears and answers his prayer. And Lehi rejoices in the promise that God's power and goodness and mercy are over all the earth and that the world will be redeemed. Yet still Lehi must leave everything and wander in the desert with his family and suffer great afflictions. And still the city of Jerusalem is destroyed.

Lehi with a book

Let's turn now to a consideration of Nephi's account in this same chapter of Lehi's second vision. Ironically, the comparative wealth of information that Nephi gives us about Lehi's second vision works, in some respects, to make it even more mysterious than the initial encounter. Nephi's elisions and omissions, coupled with the vision's own internal logic of detour and delay, compound the mute opacity of the first.

Exhausted by the Spirit, Lehi returns home from his first vision to collapse on his bed. Overcome, he is carried away in a second vision that ratchets God's initial harrowing of Lehi's body a full turn deeper, down now into his heart and into his mind. "Being thus overcome with the Spirit, he was carried away in a vision, even that he saw the heavens open and he thought he saw God sitting upon his throne, surrounded with numberless concourses of angels in the attitude of singing and praising their God" (1 Nephi 1:8). Out of these open heavens, Lehi sees "one descending," followed by twelve others. The first is brighter than the sun at noonday. The twelve that follow are brighter than the stars. The twelve scatter across the face of the earth, but the first comes straight to Lehi and brings him a book. "And the first came and stood before my father and gave unto him a book and bade him that he should read" (1 Nephi 1:11). In response, Lehi reads the text aloud and, as a result, is filled again with the Spirit of the Lord.

Next, Nephi gives what seems to be our only direct quotation from the heavenly book itself, an oracle pronouncing judgment against Jerusalem: "Woe woe unto Jerusalem, for I have seen thine abominations" (1 Nephi 1:13). Nephi then moves directly to a swift summary of the book's remaining content: "Yea, and many things did my father read concerning Jerusalem, that it should be destroyed and the inhabitants thereof; many should perish by the sword and many should be carried away captive into Babylon" (1 Nephi 1:13). Reacting to this oracle of woe, Lehi's response is surprising. Hearing it, he neither quakes nor trembles but instead shouts praises that, presumably, echo the songs of praise sung by the assembly of angels surrounding God's throne. "Great and marvelous are thy works, O Lord God Almighty," Lehi cries. "Thy throne is high in the heavens, and thy power and goodness and mercy is over all the inhabitants of the earth" (1 Nephi 1:14). Empowered to speak by the work of reading aloud, Lehi joins the heavenly choir, the divine council that is continually convened in the presence of God.

Note now a distinctive feature of this experience: there is in this vision quite a bit of what we might call "divine misdirection." Stepping back for a moment from an examination of what we *are* told by Nephi and what *is* given in the vision, we should also consider what we are *not* told and what God does *not* do. And when we do, surprising elisions and omissions (on Nephi's part) and apparently unnecessary detours and delays (on God's part) dominate the account. Consider especially one of the vision's most curious features: the whole of the vision pivots around a book that Lehi is asked to read. What is this book, and why is Lehi asked to read from it in the first place? The "one" who descends "out of the midst of heaven," whose "luster was above that of the sun at noonday," brings Lehi this book. Nephi never explicitly identifies who the "one" is—though, presumably, Nephi could have offered an interpretation, even if his father did not. Clearly, from our later perspective, the "one" is Christ and the twelve are his apostles. But it is not entirely clear, especially early on, how developed Lehi's own understanding of "a Messiah" is. In some respects, Lehi's Christology appears at this point (perhaps unsurprisingly) relatively vague and undeveloped. (We might compare, for instance, Lehi's vision of the tree of life with Nephi's expansive and detailed interpretation of that same dream.) What do we know about the "one" based just on the account? At least at the level of Nephi's narration, we are told only that the "one" descends "out of the midst of heaven" and that "his luster was above that of the sun at noonday." These two details make, I think, the "one's" most obvious prior point of reference the God who sits enthroned in the middle of the angelic throng.

But even apart from Nephi's reluctance to clearly identify the "one," a more important question remains: why, when the "one" arrives, does he bring Lehi a *book*? Why do we lack any account of the "one" communicating directly with Lehi? Why does the "one" descend from heaven in power and glory only to accomplish the mute handoff of a text? Why, if God is present *in person*, would that same God redirect Lehi's attention to the reading of a book? What's the point of this frustrating detour? Why have a text stand in for God if God is there? Is not the point of a divine text to connect you with God? Is not the book a distraction in this instance? Or, at best, redundant? (It seems a bit like being in the same room as someone you love and, then, rather than addressing them directly, insisting that you converse only by way of telephone—or, better, insisting that, though you're standing face to face, all communication be routed only through a series of elliptical text messages!)

Similarly, what about two crucial features of this second vision that Nephi *could* have presented front and center but instead omits entirely from his initial summary: (1) his delayed report that "the things which [Lehi] read in the book, manifested plainly of the coming of a Messiah and also the redemption of the world" (1 Nephi 1:19), and (2) his delayed report of Lehi's actual prophetic commission (see 1 Nephi 2:1)? Why are we told about both of these things only in passing and only after the fact? The coming of a Messiah, the redemption of the world, and Lehi's explicit commission as a prophet are not minor details. Rather, they ought to be at the center of the entire account.

Why all the detours and delays? Why all the omissions and elisions? I don't know.

But we can at least note that the imposition of such detours seems consonant with a much larger pattern. Take, for instance, the case of the Book of Mormon itself. Why go to the trouble of giving Joseph Smith the golden plates, have him translate that text with a method that hardly touches them, and then make the plates themselves disappear? Why force contemporary readers to detour through the text alone when solid evidence and a more direct connection seems possible? Why would God go out of his way to hide evidence and make his own (world-historically pivotal) message more obscure and less credible?

Or, even more to the point, what about God's own absence? Why put us in the same weak position as Lehi? Why give us a text, at least twice removed from God himself, rather than give us some kind of direct interaction with God? Is this a game or a test? Is God just testing us to see if we'll believe things that we don't have good evidence for? If this is the case, then what is God testing for, credulity? Is credulity the measure of a life, the litmus test for salvation? In effect, is God saying: "You're welcome to join me in eternal bliss, but only if you're willing to believe (in *exactly* the right way) things that I intentionally and unnecessarily made really hard to understand and believe?"

I don't buy it. I don't buy this version of the story.

Life will surely test, at every turn, our willingness to be faithful to the hard work of caring for it, but life is not itself a cosmic pop quiz. And salvation, to whatever degree we're able to receive it, is not equivalent to getting a passing grade on your super-detailed, lifelong report card.

What, then, is gained by all these detours and delays? Is there some reason why our deliverance from affliction and loss and suffering cannot just directly and definitively be a deliverance from affliction and loss? Why (as for Lehi) must we suffer the forced choice of either willing sacrifice or devastating judgment? Why not provide a third option: freedom from all that trouble and delay in the first place?

The mysteries of God

There are more questions here than answers. But even without answers the questions have force. At the very least, these questions work to bring more clearly into view what, in the very first verse of the very first chapter of the Book of Mormon, Nephi simply calls "the mysteries of God." The mysteries here in question are, on my reading, neither peripheral nor accidental. These mysteries are not an optional or temporary feature of the world. And it seems to me that, in the end, receiving God's grace and divine favor turns on our willingness to live our way *into* them.

God is, without a doubt, offering a real and present and palpable kind of deliverance from the losses and afflictions of life. But (and this is a big *but*) the *kind* of deliverance he's offering appears to depart pretty sharply from the kind of deliverance we thought we wanted. We thought we wanted the golden plates, but God gives us a little blue paperback instead. We thought we wanted to talk directly with God, but God, even when he shows up in person, asks us to read something instead. We thought God might spare Jerusalem, but God asks us to willingly flee it instead.

The critical opening verse of the Book of Mormon (1 Nephi 1:1) reads as follows:

> I Nephi having been born of goodly parents, therefore I was taught somewhat in all the learning of my father. And having seen many afflictions in the course of my days, nevertheless having been highly favored of the Lord in all my days, yea, having had a great knowledge of the goodness and the mysteries of God, therefore I make a record of my proceedings in my days.

Note first the relatively elaborate structure of the verse. The verse is structured by its two repetitions of the word *therefore* and its four repetitions of the word *having*. On my reading, the verse's two *therefores*, rather than its four *havings*, are the key to its basic structure. If we give priority to the *therefores*, then the verse makes two claims that have a distinctly causal structure:

1. Having been born ... therefore I was taught.
2. Having been afflicted ... therefore I make a record.

This causal "division of labor" (X therefore Y) is noteworthy. It's Nephi's being born that leads to his having been taught, but it's his having been afflicted that leads to his being compelled to write. His writing takes place as an inscription of his suffering. We're taught because we're born, he says, and we write (we order and record and narrate and inscribe) because we suffer.

However, it's the second claim that matters most here. To this point, I've compressed the complexity of the second claim in order to draw out its parallels with the first, but three of the verse's four *havings* belong to the second claim. Of the four repetitions, "having been born" belongs to the first claim, but "having seen many afflictions," "having been highly favored," and "having had a great knowledge" all belong to the second claim. On my reading, the third and fourth *havings* condition or qualify the second. (In fact, given the *yea* that punctuates the relationship of the third to the fourth *having*, we might even read the fourth as an elaboration of the qualification initially made in the third.) Graphically, we might represent the verse's structure like this:

1. *having* been born of goodly parents, <u>therefore</u> I was taught somewhat in all the learning of my father.
2. and *having* seen many afflictions in the course of my days, nevertheless
   a. *having* been highly favored of the Lord in all my days,
   b. yea *having* had a great knowledge of the goodness and the mysteries of God, <u>therefore</u> I make a record of my proceedings in my days.

Nephi's claim to have seen many afflictions in the course of his days is conditioned and qualified by his having been highly favored and having had great knowledge. And most importantly, the relation of these two qualifications to his having seen many afflictions is structured by the verse's key term: Nephi's *nevertheless*. "Having seen many afflictions, *nevertheless* ..."

Theologically, this *nevertheless* is pivotal. Compare, for instance, Jesus's prayer in the Garden of Gethsemane: "Father, if thou be willing, remove this cup from me: nevertheless not my will, but thine, be done" (Luke 22:42). Even given the fact that suffering and affliction condition the possibility of life and agency and love, *nevertheless* there is favor and goodness and knowledge. The *nevertheless* marks how favor and goodness and knowledge are all dependent on the experience of suffering even as they are not reducible to it. The word marks how favor and goodness and knowledge are not something detachable from loss and affliction but are dependent on a certain way of holding oneself in relationship to that suffering. This redemptive posture, this way of holding life's losses and passing, does not treat those losses simply as a negative, as a minus, as a "less." Rather, it holds life in such a way that divine favor and goodness and knowledge are not "less" (they are "never less") because of the afflictions. This recognition, the adoption of this posture in relation to suffering, is the heart of the gospel. It is what makes forgiveness and redemption possible.

In this respect, Nephi has been quite precise in this opening verse about what the mysteries of God involve. The mysteries of God have to do with this *nevertheless*. To understand the mysteries of God is to understand how it is possible to see many afflictions *and* still be highly favored. This is the mystery: God's redemption does not involve an elimination of all suffering but a transformation of our relationship to that suffering such that the suffering itself becomes a condition of knowledge and favor.

Divine favor travels a path that runs parallel to the path of loss and affliction. Responding to God's call to repent, to sacrifice, and to consecrate does not involve switching from one track to the other, from the track of suffering to the track of divine favor. Rather, it involves our commitment to both, to holding life's losses together with Jesus's *nevertheless* in a way that acknowledges the reality of our failures and losses while still trusting that life *nevertheless* is good and beautiful. At times, the parallel line of deliverance bends and directly touches the line of affliction, freeing us from that particular trouble. But often (perhaps much more often), God is working at a more fundamental level to transform our natural posture in relation to loss and affliction from one of fear and refusal to one of love and responsibility. This is the divine mystery: freeing us entirely from loss and suffering—from the necessity of sacrificing everything—would not free us from the troubles of life. It would free us only (and disastrously) from life itself.

The mystery is that having the golden plates available would not solve the real problem, that having God show up in person would not solve the real problem, and that freeing us from some particular affliction (while desirable in itself) would not solve the bigger problem. The facts of life and love inseparably entail loss and vulnerability. And the substance of both life and love is composed by the work this *nevertheless* does to weave life's afflictions and God's divine favor together. In this sense, the aim of the gospel is not simply to give us what we think we want. Rather, its aim is to show us that what we thought we wanted is not what God, in all his goodness and wisdom and mercy, is actually trying to give.

Dreams, Visions, and Foolish Imaginations: Alternative History as Sacred History in the Book of Mormon

George B. Handley

EVERY HISTORY HAS A COUNTERHISTORY. Every storyteller—intentionally or unintentionally or both—leaves behind traces and fragments, enough detritus to create entirely new and alternative narratives, narratives often taken up by a new generation or by an ostracized minority. While any given storyteller might wish to deliberately hide facts or to deceive an audience, elision lies at the heart of what it means to tell even the most truthful of stories. It is, in short, a function of the very human limitations of memory, language, and understanding. Nevertheless, these limitations are also precisely what believers often expect revelation to expunge. A revealed text is believed to be distinguished from a secular one because it descends upon us, originating in an absolute sense from outside and above the context of human language, culture, historical moment, and personality. The relative absence of strong and identifiable narrative personalities in the Bible has helped to solidify these expectations. The stories emerge as if out of the ether, leaving scholars scrambling to assemble arguments about authorship. Indeed, the work of historicizing biblical narratives has been fraught with controversy among faith communities precisely because it seems to go against the grain of our expectations for a revealed book. To personalize and historicize, let alone to pluralize narrators, is to ground voices and stories in a particular and messy context, and the perceived threat is that this work will rob the narrative of its transcendent and transferable meaning as typology.

Of course, this fear is not without grounds. Contemporary reading practices in academic circles are guided by the general assumption that truth is constructed by a series of behind-the-scenes machinations that help create the illusion of something that feels inevitable, timeless, and true but is in fact deliberate, historical, and partial. The critic's job is to expose the politics of storytelling—the elisions and distortions—that have created such an illusion. Criticism is thus a vital means of protecting readers against falsehoods and otherwise misleading meanings that stories can convey. The presumption is that such criticism seeks to lay the foundations for new meanings to emerge that are presumably more honest and transparent about narrative limitation and interest. Of course, this is often a standoff that leaves us uncertain as to how to approach sacred writ. It certainly does not seem to be desirable to raise a generation of readers who are not equipped with the requisite critical skills to protect themselves against the dangers of propaganda, but it also seems that faithful reading calls for something more trusting than a hermeneutics of suspicion. We could reconcile this dispute by saying that sacred writ deserves to be read differently than, say, the newspaper or any form of secular literature, but that only seems to dodge the question. If I do not already recognize the sacred status of a revealed book, how am I going to be sure I am not being deceived unless I employ critical distance at least in some measure?

What is curious about the Book of Mormon and the Latter-day Saint faith community is that generations of scholars have sought to authenticate the foundational narrative of the religion by means of historicizing the text—either by exegetical or extratextual (that is, archaeological) means. Historicization, in other words, is not seen as a means of debunking but of authenticating a text that has evaded definitive material evidence of its status as historical. Even Grant Hardy's recent work in trying to foreground more emphatically the narrative personalities of the book's various narrators, although seen with suspicion by some believers because it seems to bring down the heroes of the story a notch or two, is largely seen as faith promoting, rather than faith destroying, because it lends historical plausibility to the authors.[1]

For my part, I want to respond theologically to what it might mean to read such a highly mediated and overlaid narrative as the Book of Mormon.[2] The book foregrounds rather than hides the many and various personalities and interests behind its narration. That is, it wants to directly confront the fact of human personality, culture, and language and how it relates to revelation. Its radical message appears to be that our humanity is not the obstacle but rather the very medium of revelation. Although offered as a transcendent book with transferable and typological meaning, the Book of Mormon reveals divine truth paradoxically by displaying the very human process of telling stories, of rereading and reinterpreting those same stories for what they omit, and then retelling them again. The Book of Mormon, in other words, does not offer divine truth as that which transcends or bypasses the problem of human personality but as that which exposes how human interests and limitations can facilitate communication with God. The historicity of the book's narrators and editors, in other words, does not condemn them for their narcissism, blind ambition, or deception but instead reveals the power by which those weaknesses are redeemed. In revelation, human weakness becomes strong. Revelation becomes the

---

1. There is another form of historicizing that is not as warmly received among believers. I am referring, of course, to the work of some scholars who have sought to historicize the Book of Mormon in the context of nineteenth-century America and thus debunk the book's sacred status by reducing it to the psychology and life and times of Joseph Smith. However, this work, albeit motivated by a contrary view of the status of the Book of Mormon, is essentially guided by the same methodology. The only difference is the degree of its reductionism. While these attacks on the sacred status wish to reduce the entirety of the Book of Mormon to the Joseph Smith story, Mormon apologists have at least risked painting themselves into similar corners when they have argued for specific evidence—linguistic, geographical, archaeological, etc.—of the book's authenticity.

2. In this regard, I am writing in the spirit of theological inquiry modeled by Joseph Spencer's *An Other Testament: On Typology* (Provo, UT: Neal A. Maxwell Institute for Religious Scholarship, 2016).

means by which counterhistories are recovered and redeemed rather than defiantly excluded or ignored. Revelation becomes the mirror into which we look to see ourselves as well as the window through which we see the divine.

When Joseph Smith said, "We believe the Bible to be the word of God as far as it is translated correctly," he offered a famously heretical qualifier to the Bible's sacred status (Articles of Faith 1:8). He implied that God's word had been mediated by human language, modified even, perhaps to the point of losing some clarity about eternal truth, by willful even if well-intentioned men. This problem of imperfect mediation is precisely what necessitates the work of restoration. The Bible, as the Book of Mormon has famously claimed, was brought to the Americas by the Gentiles, who are simultaneously described as being favored of the Lord and as being in a "state of awful wickedness ... [stumbling] because of the plain and most precious parts of the gospel" that have been omitted by the imperfect process of human translation (1 Nephi 13:32). The Bible and the Gentiles who carry it are the imperfect means of simultaneously advancing the word of God in the Americas and causing wreckage, error, and omission. The implication is that a faithful reading of the Bible need not exclude a healthy suspicion regarding the potential presence of human personalities at work in shaping the narratives for self-interested purposes. The bold point of restoration theology is that the Bible has been tainted by the fingerprints of humanity, human culture, time, language, politics, bias, and so on.

Fair enough. But the claim is still that the Bible is the word of God, worthy of our reverent reading. We are to believe that somehow in all of that exchange of stories, values, and ideas among competing cultures, interests, and languages, the word and the will of God still manage to shine through. Joseph's claim asks us to read the Bible with one eye on the human and one eye on the divine. We need to understand, in other words, how it is that divine power and understanding might emerge *through* the complex stories of human experience and limitations of human language, not *despite* them.

I want to pause here and draw an example from the fiction of William Faulkner, because he provides an interesting case study of how we might simultaneously recognize human personality and weakness as well as divine sovereignty and purpose in the Bible. In his famous story "The Bear," two cousins engage in an important theological debate. Where is God in Southern history? How are God and the Bible still useful in the wake of a civil and racial conflict that compromised the integrity of the story Southerners wanted to tell about the divine foundations of their country? How can they reconcile God with a history that is full of human suffering and error? One of the cousins, McCaslin, notes that since the Bible was read to justify slavery, perhaps it is no longer useful. Ike responds to this criticism by saying, "There are some things He said in the Book, and some things reported of Him that He did not say."[3] Ike's cousin responds: Doesn't this imply that "these men who transcribed His Book for Him were sometime liars"? Ike then answers:

> Yes. Because they were human men. They were trying to write down the heart's truth out of the heart's driving complexity, for all the complex and troubled hearts which would beat after them. What they were trying to tell, what He wanted said, was too simple. Those for whom they transcribed His words could not have believed them. It had to be expounded in the everyday terms which they were familiar with and could comprehend, not only those who listened but those who told it too, because if they who were near to Him as to have been elected from among all who breathed and spoke language to transcribe and relay His words, could comprehend truth only through the complexity of passion and lust and hate and fear which drives the heart, what distance back to truth must they traverse whom truth could only reach by word-of-mouth?[4]

---

3. William Faulkner, *Go Down, Moses* (New York: Vintage Books, 1994), 246.
4. Faulkner, *Go Down, Moses*, 246–47.

Faulkner's notion of revelation here is deeply and richly confused with the workings of the human imagination and human desire. For one, biblical language never shakes off the dust of "word-of-mouth" orality; it always emerges and makes meaning in the sweaty and dirty context of specific human lives. Textual weaknesses are our human weaknesses reflected back to us since the "truth" speaks only after translating the language of the heart ("passion and lust and hate and fear") into "everyday terms." Instead of direct and transparent transcribers of God's word, the authors of the Bible are translators, engaged in finding a new language of their own for what is intuited by the heart. The complexity of the confusion is evident in the fact that this translation apparently must "lie" in order to speak the truth, by which Faulkner means that revealed truth is always spoken indirectly, refracted through culture, like any great work of literature. This in turn implies that sacred literature is perhaps not categorically different from other kinds of storytelling and that our understanding of scripture would benefit from both trustful *and* critical reading. As I have suggested, this is not unlike what Joseph Smith's statement about the Bible asks of us.

When Joseph Smith spoke of the Book of Mormon, at first glance it appears that he was suggesting that the Book of Mormon avoids these dilemmas altogether because of the divine nature of the translation. No qualification about correct translation is apparently necessary. Indeed, in the very introduction to the Book of Mormon, we read his words: "I told the brethren that the Book of Mormon was the most correct of any book on earth, and the keystone of our religion, and a man would get nearer to God by abiding by its precepts, than by any other book." Of course, to say that it is the "most" correct book is to admit that it is not entirely without error; it simply means that it has fewer errors. Whatever those errors might be, they do not seem to be enough to obstruct the book's power to bring its readers nearer to God. So should those errors not concern us? Does the Book of Mormon stand apart because it does not reach the threshold of sufficient numbers or kinds of error to lead us astray? In other words, are we to assume there are no such traces in an almost perfect translation? Should we ignore the traces of stories that are buried in the narrative, deliberately or inadvertently omitted, skillfully and even artfully cast aside in order to forge

piritual power? Does the power thus forged justify the omissions?
ould we disregard the human personalities that motivate the stories
told? If so, what is our theology that presumably renders narrative personality irrelevant?

I want to argue that the Book of Mormon brings its reader to Christ precisely because of its human fingerprints. The Book of Mormon highlights itself as a divine work mediated by human language and culture. Despite its stark and even exceptional differences with the Bible in the means of its transmission and translation, it paradoxically even more emphatically foregrounds how revelation comes through human language, is interpreted in human contexts, and is therefore never completely independent of human personality. So, if Faulkner's take on the Bible might seem heretical from the perspective of strict fundamentalism, it seems well suited to a book that announces in its very first pages and throughout that it is the product of very human personalities and a long and protracted process of telling and retelling, of selectively editing, cutting, and highlighting according to both human and divine interests. We are even going to discover that the first pages we are reading stand in the stead of a text already absented by human error, the lost 116 pages from the record of Lehi. Not only are the golden plates missing, but so is the record of the dream we are reading about.

What gives the Book of Mormon its revelatory and redemptive power is not the fact that it is untainted by human interest but that it reveals human interest as that which can facilitate and mediate, rather than obstruct, divine revelation. The book asks: Can God reveal himself in the intricacies and particulars of our lives—in the partiality, imagination, and willfulness of our hearts—even when or if our narratives about divine intervention remain shaped by our human interest and culture? The Book of Mormon emphatically insists that God can do so, as long as we are willing to embrace revelation as ongoing.

The Book of Mormon announces that it is a history and a record of revelations given to a small band of wanderers, unnamed and unknown in the Bible, who departed from Jerusalem around 600 BC, who arrived in the New World, and who therefore represent just one of many stories of divinely guided peoples not included in the Bible. It is, in other words, an alternative history that does not seek to compete with or undermine the Bible but rather to corroborate, complete, and fulfill it. It does not offer itself as the final word, however, or as a book with no elisions. It simultaneously points to other books yet to come forth and highlights the role of redaction—highly selective editorial work—in its own production. It suggests that because the ultimate and final restored truths of God and of history are always buried beneath many layers of the mediation of human culture and language and interest, we must not be satisfied merely with what we already know. We will end up like Christ's disciples in the Old World and think we know all that is necessary (keep in mind that in 3 Nephi 15:18, Christ describes them as guilty of "stiffneckedness and unbelief") unless we are assiduously committed to seeking out and even imagining when necessary the fragments of human stories that are left out. We must read every story for what it reveals but also for what it obscures, because beneath each remembered and recounted story lie countless others, as numberless as the sands of the sea, indeed, as many as the seed of Abraham. The first chapter of the Book of Mormon, 1 Nephi 1, illustrates just this point. It demonstrates our need to be reading as much for what it tells us as for what it does not tell us.

When you open the Book of Mormon, you might expect an omniscient narrator, like we find in Genesis, but we learn immediately that a man, not God, is speaking, and a particular man at that. We are reading a spiritual autobiography. "I Nephi," he announces, "having been born of goodly parents," write to you, dear reader, in a particular "language of the Egyptians" that is also shaped by the "learning of the Jews" on plates that I have made "with mine own hand" (1 Nephi 1:1–3). The mediation of his language, his story, and his hand is not what obstructs the revelations we will read, but it is instead announced as the means of transmission. Nephi's hand is literally made evident in the telling. In fact, he says that he knows that the record he creates is true because "I make it with mine own hand, and I make it according to my knowledge" (v. 3). The focus here is on the "madeness" of the record; it is made by human hands and according to human understanding. And Nephi insists that he knows it is true because of its construction by his hand and knowledge. His historicity—his personality, in other words—are central to the book's truth claims.

It is as if the text must confess its human weakness in order to reveal its divine strength. This conversion has much to do with the ways in which his language points to particulars that are now absent. For example, Nephi's hand, his voice, and his record stand in the stead of an absent record of his father. Moreover, as we read, his words stand in the stead of his very hands that write them. And, of course, we read a translation of a record that is also missing. The problem of human mediation is, in other words, front and center, but if we are to get to God's truth, it won't be because human language gives us unmediated access to the lost signifier. Instead, it will be by means of missing media, since his hand, his original language, Lehi's record, and the plates themselves are all absent. It is as if he opens the record saying, "You can no more see the evidence of the truthfulness of this book than you can see my hand." All language is mediated and it is all missing its original medium. From the outset and consequently throughout, the Book of Mormon announces itself as both a historical record and a metatext, as a self-consciously crafted, edited, revised, and selected text, mediated, protected, and perpetuated by the thick personalities of particular men.

Nephi complicates things further. The very genesis of his record is a vision that motivates his family's departure from Jerusalem. This vision, however, like his hand, is something already and always mediated by reported speech and reported events redacted by Nephi, who tells us that we are reading his "abridgment of the record of my father" (1 Nephi 1:17). However—and this is crucial—the very purpose of the redactions is to bring us closer, not to push us farther away, from revelation. As he later explains in chapter 6:

> And it mattereth not to me that *I am particular to give a full account of all the things of my father*, for they cannot be written upon these plates, for I desire the room that I may write of the things of God. For the fullness of mine intent is that I may persuade men to come unto the God of Abraham and the God of Isaac and the God of Jacob, and be saved. Wherefore the things which are pleasing unto the world I do not write, but the things which are pleasing unto God and unto them which are not of the world. (1 Nephi 6:3–5)

So while the Book of Mormon attracts attention from apologists and critics alike for its debatable historicity and the debatable status of the original plates, the text itself is already foregrounding the problem of a missing medium. Lehi's vision—the book's "first vision" as it were—lies at the heart of the civil and racial crisis that later ensues between brothers, a crisis that is essentially the result of conflicting understandings of what it means to interpret a mediated story that has lost its original medium.[5] A dream is not a lot to hang one's hat on, but Lehi's vision is analogous to the authority of the Book of Mormon itself. A dream is something already heavily mediated by the imagination of the dreamer, and his dream is reported to us second or perhaps third hand. Lehi had it, wrote it down, and Nephi is remembering and reinterpreting it. The mediated dream leaves us to make our own wager that, with or without the original medium, revelation is either always or never mediated by human language and understanding.

What do Lehi's visions in 1 Nephi 1 reveal? It is hard to say behind the smoke screen of Nephi's words, but what we can gather is that, at first, a divine presence of some kind is made visible and audible to Lehi in the form of a pillar of fire upon a rock. "He saw and heard much" (1 Nephi 1:6), but how much or what exactly, Nephi does not tell us. Does Lehi have more to say on the subject? We will never know. What Nephi does tell us, what we can see, is how Lehi was affected by what he saw and heard: "He did quake and tremble exceedingly" (v. 6). Nephi leads us with Lehi back to his house, where "he cast himself upon his bed, being overcome with the Spirit and the things which he had seen" (v. 7). In that state—perhaps now a state of dreaming, we are not sure— the sublime intensity of the vision begins to gain coherence and grow in content even as it moves further away from the more unmediated and empirical moment of the initial vision. He sees God on a throne,

---

5. I should note that, like Faulkner's fiction and the fiction of a great many New World writers, the Book of Mormon directly addresses the context of the nations of the Americas—where they have all suffered civil and racial strife that stems from competing interpretations of history and of the meaning and the will of the divine, and where reconciliation and the forging of new communities have resulted only from a willingness to recognize how the disparate constituencies of emerging democracies in the Americas are not secondary or tangential but centrally important to the national story.

surrounded by praising angels in the "attitude" of singing (v. 8), a rather static vision at first, like a black-and-white photograph of divine presence. But then, as the dream deepens, it gains detail and action. He sees "one" (v. 9; capitalized in later editions with the obvious intent to indicate Jesus) "descending out of the midst of heaven" and "twelve others following him" to go "forth upon the face of the earth" (vv. 10–11). By this point, we expect some grand announcement, some specification. Who is this "one"? What is he going forth to do or to say? Who are the twelve? Of course, to a contemporary reader, these are only rhetorical questions. We think we know, but it still begs the question: Why the vagueness, why the abstract "one"? Was Lehi not sure who this messiah was? Did he not yet understand his own commission? Did the dream merit multiple retellings before it could gain more content and portent? Is the vagueness here a signal of the way in which records, passed on from one generation to the next, inevitably take on meaning and attributes that stem from the hermeneutical task of intergenerational interpretation? What is perhaps most stunning about this revelation is what it simultaneously conceals. The "one" presents Lehi not with a discourse or a spoken prophecy, but with "a book and bade him that he should read" (v. 11). The great message of the revelation is to read, to return to the mediation of texts rather than to listen directly to God's speech. And what the book says is not directly recorded by Lehi in what we read and only partially reported by Nephi. Just as all stories require retellings, all interpretations fall short and require another attempt. Rather than bypassing this problem of perpetual rereading that interpretation entails, the vision reveals hermeneutics as the cross we must bear in our access to Christ. And my point here is that the Book of Mormon, rather than running from this problem, seems instead to make it a central feature of what it must mean to have the book in our hands.

The only specific prophetic content we get from Lehi's reading of the book is that Jerusalem has acted wickedly and will definitely be destroyed (see 1 Nephi 1:13). He rejoices in knowing that the Lord has given him and his family an escape from this fate (see v. 14). This is the reason the Lord later gives Lehi—again in a dream—the commandment that he and his family should depart (1 Nephi 2:2). The journey, then, that takes Lehi away from recorded history is motivated by a visionary dream, the truth of which requires interpreting the dream as prophecy.

We must not miss the paradoxical fact that we would not know who Lehi is if it were not for this record of departure we are reading; this record, this alternative rereading of biblical history, would not have been written were it not for the history that elided, that forgot Lehi. In the same way, the revelatory nature of the Book of Mormon itself would not be known to us were it not for the secular histories that have banished such knowledge from their midst. Supernatural, revelatory dreams are explicitly prohibited by secular knowledge, as are sacred histories. As alternative histories, then, idiosyncratic and individual dreams and mediated stories of departure from official memory will always obtain as transgressive narratives whose truth status is perpetually in doubt. The wager we must be willing to make is that we can, through the medium of ourselves as interpreters, find divine direction in these human particulars. If God can speak to Lehi through books in his dreams, he can certainly speak to us through a miraculously translated book.

The alternative to this faith is the doubt of Laman and Lemuel (and at one point that of Sariah), who see their father's dreams as nothing but delusions, the "foolish imaginations of his heart" (1 Nephi 2:11). Similar to the Book of Mormon readers who want to reduce the meaning of the book to Joseph Smith's psychology and historical context, Laman and Lemuel and Sariah want to reduce the meaning of the dreams of Lehi to his own personal history and proclivities. The text has foregrounded this problem but has also shown that it is through, not around, these proclivities that revelation will come. They call him "visionary" (1 Nephi 5:2), but Lehi responds by exploiting the epithet "visionary" for its ambiguity. Yes, Lehi admits, guilty as charged: "I know that I am a visionary man, for if I had not seen the things of God in a vision, I should not have known the goodness of God but had tarried at Jerusalem and had perished with my brethren" (v. 4). It is curious that the evidence that the vision is revelatory and not delusional is an event that can only have occurred in a parallel universe, as it were; the destroyed city is yet another missing medium. His Jerusalem is destroyed only because he said it would be, not because his wife or his sons can verify it. Of course, it is not different for Laman and Lemuel, whose position vis-à-vis the past confronts the same hermeneutical dilemma. How do they know the city is not destroyed? In chapter 17 we read:

> And thou art like unto our father, led away by the foolish imaginations of his heart. Yea, he hath led us out of the land of Jerusalem, and we have wandered in the wilderness for these many years. And our women have toiled being big with child, and they have borne children in the wilderness and suffered all things, save it were death. And it would have been better that they had died before they came out of Jerusalem than to have suffered these afflictions. Behold, these many years we have suffered in the wilderness, which time we might have enjoyed our possessions and the land of our inheritance; yea, and we might have been happy. (1 Nephi 17:20–21)

But what is Laman and Lemuel's evidence for doubting this? Only counterassertion. Only doubt itself, as opposed to belief. Indeed, Nephi has told them that with enough faith, "ye shall know at some future period that the word of the Lord shall be fulfilled concerning the destruction of Jerusalem, for all things which the Lord hath spoken concerning the destruction of Jerusalem must be fulfilled" (1 Nephi 7:13). He has no more evidence than they do. *The main difference is that in refusing the wager of the dream's significance as revelation, they disqualify themselves for the chance to shape the dream's meaning.* To wager that dreams can be revelations gives coherence, shape, and redemptive meaning to what are otherwise wanderings, exile, and suffering without purpose. This debate over the status of Lehi's dream exposes the contradiction of disbelief: it cannot reject the meaning of revelation except by an appeal to the very structure of belief so rejected. It wants to rewrite the meaning of transcendent truths without having to make the wager of belief that lies at the heart of any such work of interpretation.

So the meaning of Lehi's journey—either as divinely directed escape from destruction and sojourn to a promised land or as directionless and mad wandering—remains in the hands of the interpreters of Lehi's dreams; it is not determined by the dreams themselves. In other words, because the vision is mediated but the medium is perpetually missing, its status is subject to and requires faith. Lehi's potential for delusions is precisely what facilitates revelation. Here, a person not given to dreaming or with an inactive imagination is in a weaker position for receiving revelation than one who is.

It should also be noted that what such faith requires is an enormous sacrifice of temporal comforts, including the comfort and security of living within the accepted narratives of one's culture, anonymous and invisible, without knowledge of one's own particular genealogical travails. One's disposition toward such sacrifice is the key. The courage to depart is to risk oblivion, but it is also the courage to begin history over, to rewrite the story, maybe even to redeem history. When speaking to the poor who have been rejected from the synagogues, Alma says that it would have been better had they been humbled by the word of God than by their circumstances, but he nevertheless says that their contextually induced humility will still do (Alma 32:12–13). In other words, if cultural context—the particulars of language, social standing, historical moment, family circumstance—induces humility or in any other way induces faithful reception of the word, those particular conditions of weaknesses become strengths. Our personalities, language, and context, rather than condemning us, are redeemed as means to the end of casting us onto the shores of the Lord. Rather than obstructing our chances of drawing nearer to God, our human weakness can facilitate our reception of what God wants to reveal.

This seemingly messy blend of human circumstance and divine will is precisely what both a strict secular skepticism and a strict fundamentalist belief toward revelation cannot tolerate. These are positions that deserve and perhaps even depend on each other. And neither position, the Book of Mormon suggests, is well equipped to receive revelation. To receive Lehi's revelation for its mere content and not for its portent would be to not understand it fully enough to make use of it, which is not that different from disbelieving it altogether. In either case, it is not heard for what it is: a revelation of God's truth and a simultaneous reburial of that truth within the particulars of human language.

Nephi models what we should do when confronted with this paradox that inheres in this book in our hands. Only when it is received, retold, reimagined, and prayed over again by readers who seek their own re-visions does a vision undergo a kind of rebirth or resurrection, shedding its skin as a merely human fiction and taking on revelatory qualities. Recall that, as with Joseph Smith himself, the Lord has to speak to Lehi several times, in different ways, for him to come to understand that he has not merely imagined things. His is a gradual maturation to the point of being able to conceptualize and articulate what the Lord would have him know. He has to read a book that he himself has translated in order to understand what the Lord is trying to tell him, and Nephi has to reread and retell Lehi's words, many times—to us, to his brothers, and even, in his conversation in 1 Nephi 11, to the Lord—until it assumes a status as a magnified and redeemed version of his father's experience. Now, I do not mean to suggest it is *finally* redeemed. It is not as if it were previously condemned by its limitations and now rescued pure and clean without the taint of Nephi's interest. Rather, the dream has been repurposed—made usable by a new generation and offered to future generations with narrative overlays that extend, amplify, and reinterpret what it means. In this way, the transmission of Lehi's dream teaches us how to read, why to read, and why we should embrace our human conditions and make use of them to facilitate new understandings in new contexts.

If the messiness of this process bothers us, if we would prefer a simpler model of God's revealed word coming down to us once and for all time, why bother with any additional scripture at all? We must agree with our critics, then, and believe that there can be only one book for all time and no need for any more, or—just as despairing—believe that there is no book at all that could ever contain revelation, that no human mind, no human word could possibly capture the divine. But if we are going to insist on *continuing revelation*, we must recognize that its continuation is necessitated and facilitated by our own historicity. It is made necessary again and again by the fact of our human immersion in the language, culture, and understandings of our given times. These markers of our human moments and personalities are our limitations, but they become our strengths if we are prepared to wager belief and act on what the Lord will ask of us.

The question posed by 1 Nephi 1 is, what will you do with the revelation that lies in your hands, with the book you have been challenged to read? Are you concerned that the contents of the book are already too distant from their divine author and origin, too deeply embedded in and mediated by human language to bring you to God? Will you disbelieve it and assume that it becomes inevitably more distant, more vague, more lost to time and distorted by human personality as it moves away from its origin into your hands? Will you allow yourself to be filled with an endless nostalgia for the missing plates, the missing records, the missing hands of its authors, and fail to assume your responsibility to make the book meaningful? If you are so unbelieving in humanity and divinity alike, then what are the grounds for your belief in your own confidently dismissive interpretation?

The irony is that this deeply suspicious approach to reading leads to interpretations that are far more despairing of the human condition than their confidence in their own critical suspicion would seem to allow. The hopeful message of the Book of Mormon is that there is something redeeming, atoning, and healing about discovering our interdependency with each other and with the Lord in being able to understand revelation. There is indeed something more correct (if not perfect or final) about interpretations that recognize the need to be plural and multigenerational, as the Book of Mormon makes clear. I do not mean that we are obligated to believe in a perfectly linear and progressive understanding of revelation as it moves across cultures and generations. All interpretations enact their own omissions, including our own. But I do believe we are obligated to believe that all revelations, though requiring our devoted, faithful, and loyal attention, are contingent. Our faithfulness to the word is not diminished by this admission. It is diminished by a refusal to accept the responsibility that its contingency implies: to engage in the exhaustive effort of reading revelations carefully, interpreting them with others, and sharing and transmitting them. Such work also inevitably leads to conflict over interpretation, and this is no insignificant matter. These conflicts, as the Book of Mormon suggests, can grow to the point of violent civil conflict, racial and social oppression, and poverty. But it is a messiness that must be met by patience and forbearance rather than by violent intolerance.

Just as Laman and Lemuel's disbelief spurs Nephi on to deeper levels of revelation—revelation that ultimately reaches their posterity—the only solution to bad readings is to read again, to read more, and to read better. Our only escape from conflict and tribalism is to learn to read with enough charity to understand and extend a revelation's universal relevance beyond our own small set of circumstances. Such charity is manifested by a strong commitment to reading, to dialogue with others, and to God, who we trust can aid us in seeing, and ultimately reading beyond, ourselves.

Potent Messianism: Textual, Historical, and Theological Notes on 1 Nephi 1:18–20

Joseph M. Spencer

ACCORDING TO A READING I WILL DEFEND IN THIS ESSAY, it appears that Lehi, when he "went forth among the people and began to prophesy" (1 Nephi 1:18), addressed two distinct prophetic messages to his Jerusalem audience.[1] The first of these messages concerned things then present: Lehi is said to have testified of the "wickedness" and "abominations" of his contemporaries (v. 19). But the second message concerned things then still in the future: Lehi preached of the coming of "a messiah" as well as "the redemption of the world" (v. 19). Further, as I will suggest, these two distinct prophetic messages seem to have sparked two similarly distinct responses. When told of their wickedness, those at Jerusalem responded with mockery; when told of messianic redemption, they responded with anger. In fact, they "sought [Lehi's] life, that they might take it away" (v. 20). Direct prophetic accusation provoked only laughter and derision, but abstract and largely theological prophetic talk provoked murderous rage.

---

1. Like others in this volume, I draw all quotations of the Book of Mormon from Royal Skousen's *The Book of Mormon: The Earliest Text* (New Haven: Yale University Press, 2009), though, where it seems to me helpful to do so, I replace Skousen's suggested punctuation of the text with my own.

In the first section of this paper, I will defend the above reading at the exegetical level. However, if the narrative of 1 Nephi 1 *does*, in fact, distinguish between Lehi's accusatory preaching and his prophetic message, and if the same narrative presents blithe mockery and violent anger as distinct respective responses to these two sorts of prophetic preaching, then verses 18–20 are odd. One would expect that confrontation and accusation would invite anger and violence, while talk of some distant messianic redeemer would provoke little more than laughter. Today, to be sure, we mock wild-eyed figures that announce the world's end and reserve our political rage for those who oppose and accuse us. But historical study of the political climate of the late seventh and early sixth centuries before Christ helps to clarify why talk of messianic redemption—especially in Lehi's indefinite formulation: "a messiah," rather than "the Messiah"—might have been regarded with violent suspicion in the place and time of Lehi's preaching. It may be that, historically speaking, there is nothing at all surprising about what verses 18–20 claim. Such seems to me the upshot of the best historical research on preexilic Judean politics and religion. In the second section of this paper, therefore, I attempt to explain the basic narrative of Lehi's preaching by looking to history.

However, if history can help to clarify the basic stakes of the narrative report of verses 18–20—clarifying for modern readers what would have seemed natural in ancient times—it must be said that this only sets the stage for genuine theological reflection. In a book intentionally directed to readers living after the rise of secularism, when messianic talk is universally regarded with skepticism, it is necessary to go at least one step beyond historical reflection. If part of what makes scripture scripture is the way it reorganizes history according to patterns that outline a life lived faithfully before God, it is necessary to consider the theological measure of Lehi's messianic preaching. What could talk of an indefinite, singular messiah—Lehi's talk of "a messiah" rather than of "the Messiah"—mean for the modern reader? In what way, if any, is this brief report on Lehi's preaching relevant? Sustained reflection on Lehi's prophetic gesture helps to produce a crucial theological reconceptualization of the messianic, laying the groundwork for a notion that I will call "potent messianism." In a third and final part of this paper, therefore, I outline a theology of potent messianism, a thinking of the singular messiah.

Textual matters

The basic interpretation of 1 Nephi 1:18–20, from which I take both my historical and my theological bearings, is not currently represented in secondary literature on the Book of Mormon. In fact, so far as I have been able to find, only one author has even hinted at the possibility that Nephi means to distinguish between two sequences or subjects of prophetic preaching and two respective responses to such preaching.[2] To a certain extent, this lack in the literature seems to be a consequence of the fact that close interpretive study of the Book of Mormon is largely nascent, not yet a discipline in its own right. However, other forces may also be at work. As I read and reread this passage in current and recent editions of the Book of Mormon, I suspect that this lacuna in interpretation is largely due to the modern textual apparatus through which 1 Nephi 1 is today presented. More specifically, the current chapter and verse breaks in this case divert the reader's attention from a theologically crucial implication of the text.

There is in fact much to learn from paying close attention to the logic of the current chapter and verse breaks in the Book of Mormon. They were introduced into the text in the 1870s by Orson Pratt, who was given the task of producing an edition of the Book of Mormon that looked more like the Bible and that could be referenced more easily.[3] Before Pratt's work on the text's apparatus, the Book of Mormon was printed in simple, unnumbered paragraphs, which appeared in chapters that were generally much longer than the chapters in more recent editions of the book.[4] Royal Skousen has shown that the original

---

2. See Hugh Nibley, *An Approach to the Book of Mormon*, 2nd ed. (Salt Lake City: Deseret Book and FARMS, 1979), 40.

3. For a short overview of Pratt's work, see David J. Whittaker, "'That Most Important of All Books': A Printing History of the Book of Mormon," *Mormon Historical Studies* 6 (Fall 2005): 116–17.

4. It should be noted that the Community of Christ—and before it, the Reorganized Church of Jesus Christ of Latter Day Saints—retained the original chapter breaks in

pre-Pratt chapter breaks were part of the dictated text of the Book of Mormon and were apparently intended elements of the text.[5] When Pratt set to work both imposing shorter chapter lengths on the text and inserting relatively natural verse divisions into the text, he was faced with an essentially *interpretive* task. The chapter breaks and verse divisions that appear in current and recent editions of the Book of Mormon thus tell us something about how at least one close reader—perhaps the nineteenth-century's most dedicated student of the Book of Mormon—made sense of the text. Studying them closely also reveals how verses and chapters might have been divided differently.

These considerations are doubly relevant to the interpretation of 1 Nephi 1:18–20. First, it should be noted that what is now 1 Nephi 1 was originally only a part—a relatively small part—of a longer chapter. What was in Joseph Smith's dictation "Chapter I" of "The First Book of Nephi" is now 1 Nephi 1–5, a complicated narrative that begins with Lehi's inaugural vision of a prophecy-inspiring record (the heavenly book) coming down to him from God's presence and ends with Lehi's subsequent experience of a prophecy-inspiring book (the brass plates) coming down to him from Jerusalem. When Orson Pratt decided to break this originally integral story into five parts—each of today's first five chapters of 1 Nephi—he presumably felt he had found relatively natural breaks in its complicated narrative. One might suggest, however, that it would have been more natural to conclude 1 Nephi 1 with what is now verse 17, so the story of Lehi's preaching in verses 18–20 would have served chiefly as an introduction to the story of Lehi's departure into the wilderness.[6] Pratt's decision to place verses 18–20 in chapter 1, however, distances Lehi's preaching and Jerusalem's

---

their printings of the Book of Mormon, even after they too introduced versification into the volume. Recent republications of pre-Pratt editions of the Book of Mormon are also available, most accessibly in Joseph Smith Jr., *The Book of Mormon*, ed. Laurie Maffly-Kipp (New York: Penguin, 2008).

5. See Royal Skousen, *Analysis of Textual Variants of the Book of Mormon*, 6 pts. (Provo, UT: FARMS, 2004–2009), 44.

6. In fact, a host of textual connections between 1 Nephi 1:1–3 and 1 Nephi 1:16–17 suggests that what is now 1 Nephi 1:1–17 forms a kind of coherent textual unit, something that can be taken independently of the rest of 1 Nephi 1–5.

reaction to it from the subsequent commandment to leave the city. That decision, importantly, makes verse 20 the conclusion of what is now the opening chapter of the Book of Mormon, a fact that has rather heavily influenced interpretation of both Nephi's writings and the Book of Mormon as a whole. Nephi's reference in that concluding verse to the Lord's tender mercies assisting in the deliverance of the faithful has been taken as a kind of thesis statement both for Nephi's record and for the Book of Mormon as a whole.[7]

A second point of importance here concerns the verse divisions Pratt imposed on the text today known as verses 18–20, regardless of whether the passage should be included with chapter 1 or chapter 2. Pratt might have easily divided the passage into as many as five verses, perhaps (inserting my own verse numbers) as follows:

> [18] Therefore, I would that ye should know that after the Lord had shewn so many marvelous things unto my father, Lehi—yea, concerning the destruction of Jerusalem—behold, he went forth among the people and began to prophesy and to declare unto them concerning the things which he had both seen and heard.
>
> [19] And it came to pass that the Jews did mock him because of the things which he testified of them, for he truly testified of their wickedness and their abominations.
>
> [20] And he testified that the things which he saw and heard, and also the things which he read in the book, manifested plainly of the coming of a messiah, and also the redemption of the world.
>
> [21] And when the Jews heard these things, they were angry with him—yea, even as with the prophets of old, whom they had cast out and stoned and slain—and they also sought his life, that they might take it away.

---

7. For a good example, see James E. Faulconer, *The Book of Mormon Made Harder: Scripture Study Questions* (Provo, UT: Neal A. Maxwell Institute for Religious Scholarship, 2014), 13–14.

²² But behold, I, Nephi, will shew unto you that the tender mercies of the Lord is over all them whom he hath chosen, because of their faith, to make them mighty, even unto the power of deliverance.

As it is, however, Pratt divided the above material into only three verses, grouping what I have parsed as verses 19 and 20 into a single verse (current verse 19), and grouping what I have parsed as verses 21 and 22 into a single verse (current verse 20). Pratt's versification has, I think, determined how readers today understand the heavily abridged narrative set forth in the text. Where division into five verses might have signaled to readers that there were two distinct sequences of Lehi's prophetic preaching (my verses 18 and 20) and that each sequence produced a different response in Lehi's hearers (my verses 19 and 21), the division into three verses has caused readers to see in Lehi's preaching a single message that, consequently, solicited a largely undifferentiated response.[8]

It is worth asking what exactly may have led Pratt both to end chapter 1 where he did (immediately after Nephi's talk of tender mercies and deliverance) and to divide Nephi's summary narrative of Lehi's preaching as he did (into today's verses 18, 19, and 20, rather than in some other way). As regards the first of these interpretive moves, it seems that Pratt was attuned to the important difference between two distinct rhetorical modes operative from the beginning of the writings that appear under Nephi's name. Most often in 1 Nephi, the reader encounters a narrator's voice that describes events in the narrator's own past. Occasionally, though, the text replaces reported narration with a rather different style of discourse: the author addressing himself to his reader and describing his intentions with the record he is writing.[9] Over the course of what is now 1 Nephi 1, there is a kind of

<hr>

8. For a good example, see Brant A. Gardner, *Second Witness: Analytical and Contextual Commentary on the Book of Mormon*, 6 vols. (Salt Lake City: Greg Kofford Books, 2007), 1:74–75.

9. The most sophisticated study of Nephi's authorial style is Grant Hardy, *Understanding the Book of Mormon: A Reader's Guide* (New York: Oxford University Press, 2010), 29–86.

alternation of these two authorial voices: in verses 1–3, Nephi addresses his reader and describes his textual intentions; in verses 4–15, Nephi exchanges direct address for narrative; but then in verses 16–17, Nephi again resumes his form of direct address and again refers to his record. These several sequences of 1 Nephi 1 are rather easy to classify, as is the long narrative sequence beginning in what is now 1 Nephi 2:1 and running through the end of what is now 1 Nephi 5.

Much more ambiguous is 1 Nephi 1:18–20. This sequence largely contains narrative, but it opens with Nephi directly addressing his readers ("I would that ye should know that …") and ends with Nephi again directly addressing his readers ("I, Nephi, will shew unto you that …"). Given that the narrative report provided between these two instances of direct address is startlingly brief, it might be best to see verses 18–20 as a continuation of, rather than a break from, verses 16–17 in terms of their rhetorical mode.[10] Pratt, it would seem, felt it better to couple what is now verses 18–20 with the rest of what is now 1 Nephi 1 than to make it a rhetorically awkward overture to the uninterrupted narrative sequence of what is today chapters 2–5.[11] Moreover, this had what Pratt may have seen as the added benefit of allowing Nephi's forceful claims regarding what he hopes to "show" his readers to be highlighted by their conclusive position at the end of today's chapter 1.

As regards Pratt's division of verses 18–20 into distinct verses, it might be suggested that Pratt was well accustomed to the more general rhetorical style of Nephi's writing. Pratt seems to have divided what is now verse 19 from what is now verse 18 because of the "and it came to pass" that opens the former. There is no mistaking that throughout the writings attributed to Nephi, this well-worn Book of Mormon formula

---

10. The fact that Nephi uses the word *behold* in the course of his summary may be important. In the narrative report of this chapter, Nephi uses this rhetorical gesture only when directly addressing his readers. This may suggest that he means to provide in verses 18–20 not so much a narrative as a portrait of Lehi's preaching. He asks his readers to behold something, rather than to follow the "it came to pass" formulae that track the progress of a narrative.

11. Likely, Pratt also meant to group together all of Lehi's actions in Jerusalem in chapter 1 and all of Lehi's actions in the wilderness in chapter 2.

narks progress in narrative sequences of the text. Halfway through what is now verse 19—where, as I suggested above, one might have expected Pratt to start another verse—Pratt seems to have seen enough continuity to resist the temptation to impose a division. Interestingly, if there is a distinction being drawn in the text between Lehi's preaching of repentance and Lehi's preaching concerning a messiah, the text does not indicate it by employing the usual "and it came to pass." Instead, halfway through verse 19 is a simple "and" ("and he testified that … "). Pratt seems to have taken the missing "and it came to pass" to indicate that all of what is today verse 19 reports on a single event, rather than on what I suggested above might or even should be regarded as distinct sequences of preaching. Pratt did divide what is now verse 20 from what is now verse 19, despite the fact that it too opens without an "and it came to pass" formula. Yet there is nothing surprising about this division, since the first part of what is now verse 20 clearly begins a new sentence that moves away from the narrative report of verse 19. Why, though, did Pratt not divide what is today verse 20 into two distinct verses? He might well have done so, beginning with the "but, behold" positioned halfway through the verse. Yet it seems that he saw the close connection between Nephi's intentions to show his readers something about deliverance (the second half of today's verse 20) and the report concerning the mortally dangerous circumstances in which Lehi found himself (the first half of today's verse 20). It would seem that Pratt wanted to highlight that connection rather than allow readers of the Book of Mormon to take the last part of verse 20 as a more general statement.

Orson Pratt would thus seem to have had his reasons, all of them justifiable and in many ways insightful, for giving the shape he did to the last part of 1 Nephi 1. The question, however, is whether the interpretive tendencies that result from Pratt's imposed apparatus are themselves ultimately justifiable. Is it indeed best to take Nephi's talk of tender mercies and deliverance as a rather general thesis statement, meant to guide the reader's interpretation of Nephi's writings as a whole—or even of the Book of Mormon as a whole? And is it indeed best to infer from the text that Lehi's preaching was relatively monolithic and that little needs to be said about why two different reactions to his preaching are reported? Whether Pratt foresaw that his work on the text's apparatus would shape interpretation along these lines, it seems to have done so, and it is necessary to ask whether such interpretations constitute the best reading of the text.

Although I think good theological work can be done beginning from the idea that verse 20 lays out a kind of thesis statement for the whole of Nephi's writings—a good example of which can be found in Miranda Wilcox's contribution to this volume[12]—I think that Nephi's words are probably best read as introducing only, or at least principally, the long narrative sequence that now makes up 1 Nephi 2–5. Not only does the narrative immediately go on to report the deliverance of Lehi from his would-be murderers in Jerusalem, it goes on at much greater length to report the complex deliverance of Nephi—and his brothers— from Laban. When, in what is today 1 Nephi 5, Nephi and his brothers return to camp after their dangerous encounters with Laban, Nephi provides a brief account of how their return proved to his mother ("now I know of a surety") that the Lord gave her sons "power whereby they could accomplish the thing which the Lord hath commanded them" (v. 8). These words echo not only Nephi's famous announcement of his intentions to be faithful in 1 Nephi 3:7 but also the apparent thesis statement of 1 Nephi 1:20, which speaks of God's tender mercies "mak[ing] them mighty even unto the power of deliverance." Moreover, that such tender mercies are granted only to those "chosen because of their faith" is echoed in the last words of what is today 1 Nephi 5: "thus far I and my father had kept the commandments wherewith the Lord had commanded us" (v. 20). It would seem that the immediate focus of Nephi's claim about tender mercies and deliverance is the story of the retrieval of the brass plates. To see that focus may, moreover, be interpretively important, since Nephi does not claim that God simply delivers in mercy but rather that God's tender mercies make the faithful mighty unto the power of deliverance. Nephi's brief words about divine mercy, if carefully read, are more suggestive of Nephi's ethically

12. For another example, see James E. Faulconer, "Sealings and Mercies: Moroni's Final Exhortations in Moroni 10," *Journal of the Book of Mormon and Other Restoration Scripture* 22/1 (2013): 8–9.

troubling slaying of Laban than of transcendent gifts of divine deliverance. Nephi received power to deliver his family, and this was itself a gift of mercy, it seems.

Much more important in the context of this essay, however, is the second question I asked earlier. Is it indeed best to infer from the text that Lehi's preaching was relatively monolithic and that little needs to be said about why two different reactions to his preaching are reported? At least a couple of points might be mentioned. Whatever reasons Pratt may have used to decide on his division of the passage into verses, the text does in fact mean to distinguish between two sorts of preaching on Lehi's part, as well as between two sorts of responses to these two sorts of preaching. For instance, verse 18 describes Lehi as initially making known only "the things which he had both seen and heard," while the second half of verse 19 describes him testifying concerning "the things which he saw and heard, and also the things which he read in the book." This repetition of "saw and heard," augmented ("and *also*") with a reference to the heavenly book read in the course of Lehi's visions, suggests at the very least an eventual addition to or a raising of the stakes of Lehi's initial form or style of preaching, if not a full exchange of one message for another. Further, the first part of verse 19 describes Lehi's hearers as responding just to "the things which he testified of them," while the last part of verse 19 and the first part of verse 20 describe the same people as responding to Lehi's testifying that his visions "manifested plainly" the messianic redemption of the world. However subtle, there is a distinction between testifying *of* and testifying *that*, between a message about the state of a certain people and a message about an event still to take place in the future. Most indicative of all, however, is the simple fact that, even if verse 19 seems to lump Lehi's apparently distinct messages together, verses 19 and 20 rather clearly indicate two drastically distinct responses on the part of the people.[13] Verse 19 discusses only mockery, but verse 20 mentions

---

13. The sketchiness of the details Nephi provides may be important here. He does report Lehi's apparently distinct sequences of preaching in the course of what is today a single verse, but it should be noted how much Nephi clearly skips over in this report. There is no information, for instance, about how long Lehi preached in Jerusalem. Between the commencement of the first year of Zedekiah's reign, mentioned in 1 Nephi 1:4,

anger and murderous intentions. If something in the text should motivate this distinction between responses, reported successively, the most obvious solution is that there is indeed a distinction between the two messages that the text seems to tie to the respective responses.

In the end, then, I think there is ample reason to believe that the portrait of Lehi's preaching in verses 18–20 is meant to distinguish between two sorts of prophetic message, as well as to associate with each of those messages a distinct sort of typical response. It is necessary, in other words, to work against the grain of our contemporary textual apparatus in order to see what is at work in the text. At any rate, it is this typology of sorts—the preaching of repentance provokes only mockery, while messianic preaching provokes anger and violence—that calls for explanation. What is messianism, if announcing one's commitment to it inspires murderous rage?

Historical matters

In Lehi's particular case, as I have already indicated, there may be historical resources for answering this ostensibly theological question. And, after all, the text of 1 Nephi 1 explicitly ties the events it recounts to a determinate geographical setting and historical period. As stated at the outset of the record, Lehi's earliest prophetic experiences were spurred by events that took place "in the commencement of the first year of the reign of Zedekiah, king of Judah" (v. 4). Although not much is known about many parts of the ancient history of Israel, a good deal is known about the time of Zedekiah—and therefore about the time of Lehi.[14] At least a preliminary answer can be given, in light of available

---

and the actual destruction of Jerusalem by Babylon, ten full years passed. Is the reader to think that Lehi preached on only a couple of occasions before he was commanded to flee Jerusalem? Or is one to believe that Lehi preached for months or even years before leaving the city? If his preaching is supposed to have gone on for some time, it would hardly be surprising to learn that his message shifted over the course of his ministry or that attitudes toward him changed as he fulfilled his prophetic tasks.

14. Several helpful summaries of research on the political and religious history surrounding Zedekiah's reign have been made available in Latter-day Saint publications.

historical sources, to the question of why Lehi's hearers would have been so outraged by his talk of a coming messiah.

Lehi lived in troubled times. Zedekiah was made king not by his own people but by a foreign power—Babylon, the very empire that would lay waste to Jerusalem a decade later. Jehoiakim, the longest-reigning of Zedekiah's several immediate predecessors, had also been a puppet king, installed, however, by Egypt rather than by Babylon. For more than a decade, in fact, the small nation of Judah had been caught in the middle of a massive showdown between two massive empires, each vying for control of the entire ancient Near East. Since the complete collapse of the Assyrian Empire over the slow course of the preceding century, the major political-historical question had been whether it would be Babylon or Egypt that would take its place as the dominant world power. Judah found itself in the worst possible geographical position during this gigantomachy: right between the advancing fronts of the two empires. Eight years before Zedekiah was placed on the throne, the balance of power shifted heavily in favor of Babylon, and Jerusalem's kings were forced to declare allegiance to the Babylonian Empire, even as they harbored hopes that Egypt would regain power. Their political alliances with Egypt eventually cost them dearly when, ten years into Zedekiah's reign, Babylon punished them by eradicating their holy city.

Perhaps what was most devastating about all these circumstances was the fact that, only a few years before the trouble began in earnest, Judah had experienced a remarkable period of political independence. After Assyria had entirely destroyed Judah's northern neighbor, the nation of Israel, and devastated much of Judah itself—the worst destruction taking place in the last decades of the eighth century BC, one hundred years before Lehi's time—the collapse of the Assyrian Empire freed Judah from foreign oppression, ushering in a brief era of remarkable prosperity. That period of prosperity, moreover, coincided with the reign of a most remarkable Judean king—the much-discussed King Josiah, "the last of the significant kings of Judah."[15] In addition

---

See especially the several essays gathered in John W. Welch, David Rolph Seely, and Jo Ann H. Seely, eds., *Glimpses of Lehi's Jerusalem* (Provo, UT: FARMS, 2004).

15. Volkmar Fritz, *A Continental Commentary: 1 & 2 Kings*, trans. Anselm Hagedorn (Minneapolis: Fortress Press, 2003), 395.

to his famous religious reform, about which Julie Smith has many illuminating things to say elsewhere in this volume, Josiah achieved remarkable success through military means in expanding Judah's borders.[16] His contemporaries clearly took him to be the greatest of Judah's kings since David, the king who, according to their tradition, first secured the nation's borders and gave the covenant people rest from their political enemies. It is most likely that Josiah understood himself to be—and that his people understood him to be—a kind of "second David," a restorer of the glory of the Davidic dynasty.[17] When Josiah's military might is considered alongside his piety and zeal for the religion of his ancestors, it is no wonder that his people saw in him the fulfillment of hopes that had lain dormant for many years. The historians of his day explicitly described him as a fulfiller of prophecy.[18] Indeed, one prophetic word that may well have been regarded during the height of Josiah's power as predicting his rise is Deuteronomy 18:15, attributed to Moses and often commented on in the Book of Mormon: "The Lord thy God will raise up unto thee a Prophet from the midst of thee, of thy brethren, like unto me." Much in the biblical accounts of Moses's ministry and Josiah's reign is written in a way to suggest a connection between the two.

Unfortunately for Judah, Josiah's reign of glory did not last. As tension between Babylon and Egypt mounted, confidence in the possibility of continued political independence and consequent religious freedom naturally began to dwindle. A dozen years before Zedekiah would be placed on the throne in Judah, two events happened that clearly dashed the overblown hopes of Josiah's people. First, Babylon had its first major military victory on the geographical line that led

---

16. Biblical references to Josiah's efforts at expansion can be found in 2 Kings 23:15–18 and 2 Chronicles 34:6–7. See the helpful summary of Josiah's successes, combined with an analysis of their relevance for the daily life of originally Northern Kingdom families like Lehi's, in Jeffrey R. Chadwick, "Lehi's House at Jerusalem and the Land of His Inheritance," in *Glimpses of Lehi's Jerusalem*, 107–10.

17. See Jacob M. Myers, *II Chronicles: Introduction, Translation, and Notes* (New Haven: Yale University Press, 1965), 205–6.

18. See especially 2 Kings 23:15–18, meant to fulfill the prophecy recounted in 1 Kings 13.

through Judah to Egypt.[19] Second, Egypt brought its military forces against Judah at Megiddo, and Josiah was killed in the course of the battle, apparently by the Pharaoh himself.[20] In the course of a single year, all the political enthusiasm associated with Josiah (heightened by the religious enthusiasm associated with the king's efforts at reform) proved to have been misguided in important ways, and Judah was forced to exchange hopefulness for a kind of hardheaded pragmatism, punctuated at dangerous moments over the ensuing decades by bouts of rash desperation.

Now, it might seem that nothing of what has just been recounted has anything to do with messianism. But in order to see just how relevant all this history is to the question of Lehi's messianism—and the violent response it apparently provoked in Jerusalem at the time of Zedekiah—it is necessary to defamiliarize messianism somewhat. Latter-day Saints tend to associate messianism only with belief in the redeeming role played in the plan of salvation by Jesus of Nazareth. To see what is at stake historically in verses 18–20, however, it is necessary to see the text through a rather different lens.

Of course, it must be said that the Book of Mormon is a deeply Christian book. Centuries before Christianity begins its historical rise in the Old World, the Nephites are granted an unmistakably Christian dispensation, thanks to startlingly specific prophecies of the coming Christ. The Nephites thus know long in advance the location of Jesus's birth and baptism; they have at least a rough sense for his ministry and his impact long before he appears; they know of and clearly anticipate the Messiah's death and resurrection; and they are even prophetically aware of the basic contours of Christian history through the Middle Ages and into the modern world. The result of all this foreknowledge is the development in the Book of Mormon of a New World, pre-Christian Christianity: a people "look[ing] forward unto the Messiah and believ[ing] in him to come as though he already was" (Jarom 1:11). Importantly, prophetic clarity regarding the nature

---

19. See Mordechai Cogan and Hayim Tadmor, *II Kings: A New Translation with Introduction and Commentary* (New Haven: Yale University Press, 2008), 300–301.

20. See Fritz, *Continental Commentary*, 410–11.

of the Christian dispensation comes already in some of the prophecies of Lehi. It is not difficult to see how familiarity with the Book of Mormon leads one to believe that pre-Christian messianic hopes should always have the kind of specific prophetic foreknowledge put on display throughout Nephite history. And several Nephite prophets—Lehi included—explicitly state that their Old World predecessors "knew of Christ" and "had a hope of his glory many hundred years before his coming" (Jacob 4:4; see also 1 Nephi 10:5; Mosiah 13:33).

In the end, however, I think it is a mistake to read the implications of the Book of Mormon always in this traditional way. While it is true that passages in the Book of Mormon occasionally project its prophets' way of understanding the Messiah onto their Old World prophetic predecessors, it is equally true that other passages complicate these projections. Nephi, for instance, explicitly distinguishes between his own people's "plainness" in prophecy from the style of Old World prophecy (see 2 Nephi 25:1–8). Presumably, it is also significant that the few decades of Nephite history portrayed in Nephi's writings are portrayed as an era of increasing specific foreknowledge of Christ's coming and ministry. This includes preliminary hints in the dreams and visions of Lehi (see 1 Nephi 1:19; 10:4–11), detailed outlines in the apocalyptic experiences of Nephi (see 1 Nephi 11:13–36), helpful additions eventually discovered in scattered brass plates texts (see 1 Nephi 19:7–14), and occasional supplements in the angelic communications of Jacob (see 2 Nephi 10:3–5). In one rather telling sequence, Lehi admits that his theological convictions are woven together with some of his own speculative interpretations: "I, Lehi, according to the things which I have read, must needs suppose..." (2 Nephi 2:17). Nephite Christology does not appear from the beginning of the Book of Mormon as a full-blown phenomenon more or less borrowed from the clear writings of the Old World prophets. Rather, it is presented as slowly developed from a number of distinct sources and clearly distinguished from what can be found in the writings available in today's Hebrew Bible.

In 1 Nephi 1:19, the indefinite article preceding the word *messiah* might provide a crucial—but subtle—hint that Lehi's early messianic preaching in Jerusalem should be understood as different from subsequent Nephite christological preaching. Lehi, the text says, "testified that the things which he saw and heard, and also the things which he read in the book, manifested plainly of the coming of *a*"—note, not *the*—"messiah" (v. 19).[21] Had Lehi's hearers in Jerusalem been universally aware of a strong prophetic tradition focused on the then-still-future coming of Jesus Christ, or even if all of Nephi's anticipated readers were to be aware of a similar tradition, then it would have made sense for the narrative to report on Lehi's prophecies regarding "*the* Messiah." As it is, the narrative reports his prophecies regarding "*a* messiah," some coming messianic figure who would pursue a program of redemption. The report of Lehi's preaching thus sounds much more like what secular historians today have to say about messianic belief in the seventh and sixth centuries before Christ than what Latter-day Saints tend to say about messianic belief before the beginning of the Christian era. Consequently, in order to produce a decidedly historical account of verses 18–20, I think it is best to trust secular historians of the ancient world about what messianic belief in Lehi's day would have looked like, rather than to interpret the text solely according to our own received expectations.

What, then, did Jewish messianism look like in the years leading up to the reign of Zedekiah? The point is not just to shift from a strictly Christian to a strictly Jewish register—that is, to bracket the Christian insistence that the Messiah came in the person of Jesus of Nazareth in order to leave open the question of when, where, and in whom the Messiah might appear. Rather, the point is to recognize that this kind of messianism, familiar from both the Christian and the Jewish traditions, would have been foreign to the inhabitants of Jerusalem in the time of Josiah. Before the Jewish exile in Babylon and its aftermath back in Palestine, messianism had relatively few of the features that came to be associated with it later. The sort of messianism that would have been known to the inhabitants of Lehi's Jerusalem would have been focused much more intensely on the promises associated with the then-still-existent Davidic dynasty than on anything else. Only after

---

21. The significance of this indefinite article (*a* rather than *the*) is all the clearer in light of the definite article attached to the other things manifested plainly in Lehi's visions: "and also *the* redemption of the world."

that dynasty had been entirely removed from power (which occurred when Zedekiah's reign came to its end) could messianic hopes take on the familiar shape they seem to have developed in the centuries following the return from exile.

It is not entirely clear when the theology attached to the Davidic monarchy came into existence (some scholars suggest that it already existed by David's time),[22] but it is clear that it was fully operative in some form by at least the end of the eighth century BC, during the prophetic activity of Isaiah of Jerusalem—in whose writings Nephi demonstrates such consistent interest.[23] Certainly by the time of Josiah, this theology had come into a kind of maturity, since it underpinned the massive history of Israel produced in that period: the books of Samuel and of Kings.[24] Nathan's oracle to David in 2 Samuel 7, in which an everlasting dynasty is promised to David, unmistakably "occupies an important position in the larger Deuteronomistic corpus"; that is, it explains the hopes associated with the Davidic dynasty within the larger historical narrative constructed in Josiah's days.[25] Because so few of David's successors lived up to the glorious precedent he had set for them, the history of the Davidic dynasty was at once a history of hopes for better times and a history of disappointments due to foreign control. It was because Josiah threw off the last remnants of the Assyrian yoke in the mid-sixth century BC that he was regarded as a kind of David reborn, a return to the golden age under Judah's first covenant-bound king.

All the hopes associated with the Davidic monarchy were messianic. The Hebrew word *mashiach* or "anointed one," from which the

---

22. See, for instance, Gerhard von Rad, *Old Testament Theology*, 2 vols., trans. D. M. G. Stalker (New York: Harper & Row, 1962), 1:39–56.

23. See the general but helpful discussion in Christopher R. Seitz, *Isaiah 1–39* (Louisville: John Knox Press, 1993), 60–75.

24. Marvin Sweeney suggests that the theological shape of the earliest Isaianic writings was determined in large part by the religious and political interests of Josiah's regime. See Marvin A. Sweeney, *Isaiah 1–39 with an Introduction to Prophetic Literature* (Grand Rapids, MI: Eerdmans, 1996), 57–59.

25. P. Kyle McCarter Jr., *II Samuel: A New Translation with Introduction, Notes and Commentary* (New Haven: Yale University Press, 2008), 217.

English word *messiah* derives, was applied from the earliest period of the Israelite monarchy to the kings. David was consistently careful to avoid raising his hand against the Lord's anointed, Saul the king (see 1 Samuel 24:6, 10; 26:9, 11, 23; 2 Samuel 1:14, 16). David was later himself called the Lord's anointed (see 2 Samuel 19:21; 22:51; 23:1), as were his successors (see throughout the Psalms, but also Lamentations 4:20; Habakkuk 3:13). Messianism before the Babylonian exile was largely a matter of trusting that one of David's royal successors would eventually measure up to his father's stature, giving Israel rest from its enemies anew. The clearest—and most likely the earliest—expression of this hope is to be found in Isaiah 9:6–7, the famous announcement of a new child being born—that is, of a new king ascending the throne and being adopted by the Lord as he fulfills the hopes of the Davidic dynasty. Summarily put, "the oracle apparently concerned the joyous announcement of the birth of a new Davidic king who would have the authority, resolve, and capacity to reverse the fortunes of Judah."[26] Long before messianism became a matter of eschatological hope—of being oriented to the arrival of a figure who would mark the end of history in some way—it was a basic trust that God would honor his covenant with David and see to Judah's deliverance from political enemies.

Because Josiah was the first Judean king since David to restore political independence and because he reconquered for Judah what had been obliterated of Northern Israel during the Assyrian conquest—all this while embodying a religious piety and ritual zeal that exceeded even that of his important predecessor, Hezekiah—it is not difficult to see that the hopes invested in his reign were essentially messianic. Indeed, Josiah's repetition and radicalization of the Hezekian reform of a few decades earlier was likely crucial to the messianic lens through which he was seen: Isaiah's messianic prophecy cited above was almost certainly originally focused on the rise of Hezekiah to the Davidic throne.[27] While it seems likely that preexilic Jewish messianism was largely a limited phenomenon in the eighth century BC, common only

---

26. Walter Brueggemann, *Isaiah 1–39* (Louisville: Westminster John Knox Press, 1998), 82.

27. See, again, Brueggemann, *Isaiah 1–39*, 82.

in the king's more intimate circles of society,[28] it seems to have become much more widely popular in Josiah's time, at the very least because of the public spectacle associated with Josiah's reform. Lehi likely reached adulthood during an era of intense messianic enthusiasm, focused heavily on the potency of the Josian monarchy.

Unfortunately, as already suggested, if Josiah was originally seen as a kind of messianic figure, he would eventually have come to be seen as a failed messiah. The unstoppable advance of Babylon's armies, combined with the surprising death of Josiah and crushed hopes for Judean independence at Megiddo, likely spoiled messianism for most of Judah—and perhaps especially for the social and political elite. Only a dozen years after Josiah's tragic death, after a succession of weak puppet kings and serious problems for Judah every time one of its kings attempted to take sides, any messianic talk—any confidence in the Davidic dynasty in any form—would have sounded downright dangerous. The historically aware and socially savvy among Zedekiah's subjects would likely have responded to any messianic anticipations with a stern warning that such nonsense had been tried and had resulted only in devastating failure. Not only had the supposed messiah of a few years earlier led to oppressive subjection rather than continued independence, but now foreign rule was complete and the political situation was dangerously volatile. Should Babylon learn that certain Judean factions hoped for messianic deliverance, armies would soon be camped outside Jerusalem, ready to replace oppressive subjection with complete obliteration.

It would thus have been one thing for someone like Lehi to claim that the Lord's covenant people had strayed in some way from the Lord. Accusations of wickedness could be laughed off—regarded as little more than the ravings of a religious factionalist. It would have been another thing entirely for someone like Lehi to claim he had plain evidence of some sort that a messianic redeemer would appear. The long-term consequences of a messianic movement in Judah would likely be irreversible, especially if it presented its teachings in a soberingly clear fashion, as Lehi's talk of "plain manifestation" would suggest

---

28. See von Rad, *Old Testament Theology*, 2:169.

he meant to do. Perhaps, then, a historical review like the one I have just provided would be enough to make the report of verses 18–20 less surprising. For Lehi to have spoken of a messiah would have been terribly dangerous in the political climate of Zedekiah's reign. That Lehi understood his announcement to have world-historical implications—after all, he announced "the redemption of the world"—would have made his message all the more potent and frightening to his contemporaries. His hearers would most likely have heard in his preaching a hope that Zedekiah would be replaced by a miraculous Judean king who would lead the Jews in a successful revolt that would mark the beginning of political independence—or even of political ascendancy. To many, it would likely have seemed better that one such wild-eyed prophet should perish than that the whole Judean nation should dwindle and perish in a sustained Babylonian siege.

Of course, given the subsequent developments of Lehi's messianic thought—his startlingly plain statement later that his anticipated Messiah would not appear for six centuries, for instance (see 1 Nephi 10:4)—it must be said that he did not at all mean to suggest what his audiences likely believed they heard in his preaching. Lehi seems to have been in the earliest stages of developing a fully Christian messianism, but his listeners likely could make little sense of his message. It took Lehi's son Nephi a fantastically detailed apocalyptic vision of the whole panorama of history even to begin to see what Lehi was after. Consequently, it would be unlikely for the average inhabitant of Zedekiah's Jerusalem to think that he or she would have had more insight into Lehi's blossoming messianism than Lehi's own son. Indeed, it is perhaps possible to suggest that Lehi's family was driven from Jerusalem toward the New World precisely because their new wine could only burst the old bottles of preexilic Jewish messianism: only in a radically new setting could a pre-Christian Christianity get off the ground. Lehi's departure from Jerusalem might well have been a theological as well as a geographical departure, in the end.

At any rate, it is along the lines I have followed here that one might begin to provide a historical explanation of 1 Nephi 1:18–20. In light of the complicated Israelite history that led up to the opening events recorded in the Book of Mormon, it is possible to make at least some preliminary sense of why Lehi's contemporaries might have been not only skeptical but also murderously angry at his messianic message. Of course, there is little reason to think that any of Lehi's hearers understood the real implications of what he preached, but given their likely misunderstanding, their reaction was not surprising.

Theological matters

Even as the preceding historical survey helps to make some sense of verses 18–20, it does not really address the theological question I posed in connection with that passage: What is messianism, if announcing one's commitment to it inspires murderous rage? All we have glimpsed in the preceding pages is why a specific sort of messianic talk—or, rather, all messianic talk interpreted in a specific way—would have caused rage for one particular audience at a particular period of time and in a particular place. But are contemporary readers of 1 Nephi 1 supposed to recognize just the historical details reviewed above and nothing more? That is to say, is the point of verses 18–20 primarily historical in the end? Are its purposes exhausted once the passage's apparent oddity is explained away? Is it enough to know that at least one kind of messianic talk caused a genuine scandal during at least one point in history, or is the intention of the text to say something more general about the nature of messianic talk, about the nature of messianism as such?

While there is no gainsaying the fact that history is important to the Book of Mormon, it must be emphasized strongly that the book does not ask its readers to see past its words and stories to whatever ancient history can be recovered from authentically ancient documents and other artifacts. The book's aim is not so much to inspire readers to determine how to explain away oddities by doing good research as it is to inspire readers to determine how the text's oddities might inform a life lived in devotion to God. It seems to me that, once basic textual and historical questions have been dealt with—however summarily, as above—the real task of reading scripture can begin: namely, to ask what the text has to say about the life of faith. Here, then, the crucial question is this: *What is at stake in the messianic such that it is so deeply potent?*

Perhaps this might be put even more directly: *Why might committed Latter-day Saints need, or at least hope, to be as much an affront to their contemporaries as Lehi apparently was to his, and what has such scandal to do with messianism?*

Of course, to make a transition from history to theology is not at all to abandon things historical. Indeed, several points from the history recounted above are of particular importance for theological reflection in this case. A first point, for instance, might be that one would do well to learn from the complex political determinations of messianism that have become clear in the preceding discussion. To speak of the messianic, it seems, is to speak of something with deeply political stakes, something whose original bearings are unmistakably political. A second and related historical point of importance qualifies this first one, however. One gathers from the historical details that messianism comes to be viewed as dangerous only after some particular messianism—the hope for a specific messiah—has been widely espoused but then proven to be a failure. In other words, the wrong or problematic rejection of true messianism seems to be connected in some way with the right or unquestionable rejection of a particular messianism. This second point might be clarified by a third one. There seems to be something crucial about the historical importance of the indefinite article in Lehi's preaching—his announcement of the coming of *a* messiah, rather than of *the* Messiah. There is, it seems, something particularly threatening in the refusal to identify the coming messiah, something dangerous about the indefinite messiah. Neither particular nor universal, the singular messiah bears a force that inspires anger and violence. Finally, this third point can be developed in light of a fourth point. What the Book of Mormon presents as right or true messianism is one that develops unforeseeably beyond its immediate setting through a series of visionary experiences that alert the prophet to problems essentially foreign to the original setting in which the messianic question is first posed. The indeterminate and conceptually indefinite messiah is one concerning which further revelation should—in fact, must—be received. Those who react violently to messianic talk therefore prove to be blind to the possibility of developing messianic thought in novel directions.

For this last part of this essay, then, I will take my theological bearings from history, beginning specifically from these four points. If one were to outline the idea of "potent messianism" (the sort of messianism that leads Lehi into his dangerous circumstances) and were to do so by drawing on the historical insights just summarized, it is possible to begin from four theological theses:

1. Potent messianism is essentially political.
2. Potent messianism is founded on the ruin of particular messianisms.
3. Potent messianism is indefinite or singular.
4. Potent messianism is revisable or, we might say, reenvisionable.

In the space that remains, I would like to begin to articulate the theological importance of these several theses.

To begin, what does it mean to say that potent messianism, as the first thesis above states, is essentially *political*? Clearly, the messianic idea has its roots in a political situation. To be a messiah is to be an anointed one—that is, to be invested with authority by the established institutional apparatus and according to the established protocol (the anointing ritual that invested kings in the specifically Israelite tradition). In the Davidic context, moreover, to be a messiah is also to be a successor or an heir—the product, therefore, of a function that assigns one a dynastic place within a genealogical history. Further, when messianism comes eventually (at the latest, by the eighth century before Christ) to be woven with expectation, being a messiah becomes a matter of repetition and restoration, of making certain forms of being-with or being-together possible anew—a certain peace and political independence. In short, to the extent that messianism has reference to messiahs, it cannot fully break with the strictly political determinations that governed the investiture of kings in the ancient Near East. To speak of a messiah at all is always to speak of a certain confidence or of certain hopes associated with either political stability or political change.

The first thesis concerning potent messianism is thus relatively straightforward. Part of what makes messianism potent is its irremediable connection to political institutions, as well as to political transformation. Weaving the religious and the political—those two taboo topics never to be broached in polite company—messianism of *whatever* sort is always already effectively potent. It is impossible to divorce messianism in any absolute sense from questions of what it means to live together. Whatever one's view of the ideal social order, there is a messiah—already established or still to come—who represents and secures its goodness. The messianic institution of ancient Israel was, arguably, originally conservative in nature, an apparatus meant to ensure the long-term preservation of a certain social order. The messianic anticipations of ancient Israel that developed over the course of the monarchy's history were, however, clearly liberal in nature, an orientation aimed at welcoming the harbinger of a social order more than just the status quo. Whether conservative or liberal (using such terms extremely broadly, obviously), one's commitments tie into some sort of messianism, it would seem. Again, then, to the extent that messianism has reference to messiahs, it cannot fully break with the strictly political determinations that governed the investiture of kings in the ancient Near East.

Messianism cannot fully break with political determinations, but it must in its most potent form be said to operate only and always at the borders of such political determinations. This, it seems, is the basic implication of the second thesis above. The determinations laid out in the preceding two paragraphs are the trappings only of certain particular messianisms that were associated first with the original Davidic monarchy and eventually with the possibility of restoring Davidic political independence and peace through the arrival of a better king. According to the second thesis, however, the most potent messianism is founded only on the ruins of such particular messianisms. The conservative messianism of the Israelite monarchy eventually gave way to the liberal messianism of Isaianic and post-Isaianic hopes. But that liberal messianism in turn eventually collapsed after investing all its hopes in the specific reigns, successively, of Hezekiah and especially of Josiah. By the time Lehi could preach a radically potent messianism, all particular messianisms had fallen apart. It was entirely clear that the monarchy as an established institution would never deliver Judah anew from its political enemies. And, after Josiah's death and the installation of a series of puppet kings, it became equally clear that there was no reason to hope for an enlightened messianic hero who would liberate Judah after turning the nation back onto the right track.

To speak in a general vein, potent messianism dawns specifically when it is no longer possible to orient one's messianism by tying the anointed one to an identifiable inherited institution or by locating the anointed one in an identifiably needed restoration. Messianism's potency reaches extreme intensity only when what is in view is no longer the stabilization or the redemption of a particular nation with its peculiar institutions. Genuinely potent messianism dawns only when what is in view is more global—"the redemption of the world," as Lehi puts it. Potent messianism, in other words, is what is glimpsed in a visionary experience that outstrips the determinations of a particular messianism that has already proven itself a failure—twice over, in fact. It is in this sense that potent messianism, while nonetheless political, cannot be reduced to any particular politics. It is what works in the interstices between actual, observable political institutions and possible, imaginable political institutions. Potent messianism is what calls for thought when both the knowably actual and the knowably possible prove themselves to be fully inadequate. Only at that point is it possible to embrace the most potent messianism, the sort of messianism that always and inherently scandalizes.

It is, of course, difficult to know what all this implies. It would seem that the potently messianic does not weigh in on political debates but rather cuts their Gordian knots. But what can that mean? It would seem that the potently messianic does not take sides but cuts diagonally across every opposition, or perhaps zigzags between opposed poles. But, again, what can that mean? It would seem that the potently messianic neither slavishly obeys nor slavishly rebels against political institutions, opting rather to subject all such apparatuses to a kind of free play. But, yet again, what can that mean? At the very least, it seems to mean something like the following. Potent messianism is so profoundly scandalous because it fails—in fact, refuses—to carve up the world according to the categories determined by everyday political discourse. Its political nature lies only in the way it produces entirely new configurations of political discourse. It is easy to mock someone who has assumed an opposing political position. But it is far more difficult to know how to deal with someone who refuses to recognize as valid either of basically opposed political positions. And the anxiety that accompanies every encounter with such a person can very quickly inspire anger and violence.

How can such a reconfiguration of political discourse be accomplished? Here, it is necessary to turn to the third thesis above, that potent messianism is indefinite or singular. Potent messianism places its hopes neither in the particular nor in the universal—neither in some specifiable individual (this or that uniquely nameable person) nor in whoever happens to fit a definite conceptual description (someone who accomplishes a specifiable set of aims). The potent messiah is neither a self-identical person nor a well-formed category. And yet—this is the difficult theological point here—the potent messiah is nonetheless an unmistakable figure of fulfillment. Every messianism dreams of fulfillment, but potent messianism dreams differently. Every specific messianism dreams of seeing the peculiar desires of a determinate political apparatus fulfilled. Potent messianism, it would seem, asks after the meaning of fulfillment without commitment to any determinate political apparatus. Fulfillment of hopes, but without particular hopes that require fulfillment—that, it seems, is the orientation of potent messianism. It dreams of fulfillment as such, fulfillment per se, fulfillment without qualification, fulfillment without end, fulfillment of life.

Crucial to understanding this point is the ability to distinguish between two philosophical concepts, often equated: that of the particular and that of the singular. Where the particular can be identified because of the weave of predicates that assigns it a place in the world— one could say that the particular is identified by the parts it plays in larger categories that allow for identification—the singular is effectively indiscernible because it suspends predication in its indefiniteness: "a messiah," still "coming," whose arrival marks "the redemption," it turns out, of the whole "world." It is thus that the word *potent* in *potent messianism* gains its true resonance. The potent messiah is the potential messiah, the messiah still-to-come, the messiah who, because not yet actual, gathers into a single figure all predicates in latent form, holding them together in a kind of infinite contradiction. With such a messiah on the horizon, anything could happen, and that is what makes potent messianism so threatening. But what is crucial is that with the full arrival of the messiah, no one thing will have happened. Instead, everything will be redeemed, the infinite contradiction being sustained indefinitely. It is only with the coming of a messiah that it is possible to speak of world redemption. The web of actual objects and actual relations making up the realm of experience, even if this realm is considered diachronically—that is, over the course of history—is nonetheless only a relatively small part of the much larger web of potential objects and potential relations. For the world to be redeemed, everything actual has to be traced back in some way to its potentialities, to what might have been.

It seems to me that it is precisely for this reason that potent messianism must be visionary, and even revisionary or reenvisionary—as the fourth thesis above states. To recognize potency or potentiality is to develop a certain ability to see, to envision, to reenvision. To see what might have been, and especially to see why that matters, requires a visionary capacity that can only be called prophetic. Those who fail to understand the message of potent messianism reject it so violently at least in part because they fail to discern radically different configurations of the real latent possibilities operative in every situation. To reject potent messianism is to fail to see—or to refuse to see—the fullness of the present. It is thus to give up on fulfillment as such, apparently because the fulfillment of this or that particular messianic hope has proven so disastrous. The fullness of the world is to be found in its potentialities, its as-yet-undetermined or indefinite possibilities, rather than in the right sorts of actualities. For this reason, it is easy to come to hate potent messianism because it is difficult to see how the failure of every actual messiah to be messianic is in fact productive, indicative that the actual cannot contain the fullness that arrives with the potent messiah. In proverbial terms, the light can shine in the darkness, but the darkness cannot comprehend it.

I am led, as I think more carefully about this fourth thesis, to believe that what is at stake in visionary experience is not at all some kind of straightforward witnessing of actual historical events that take place elsewhere or at a time different from one's own. I find myself believing that what is at stake here is rather a prophetic ability to see the potentialities of a concrete situation, to see what the apparent face of a situation masks. It is for that reason that prophecies and knowledge and languages inevitably fail, while faith, hope, and love remain. To be a prophet, it seems, is to know as well as one's contemporaries that every messianic anticipation has been and should have been dashed. But it is also to know that the despairing have nevertheless been too quick to give up on the messianic. The prophet sees something potent organizing and structuring the terrifying situation of the present, something others are far too quick to dismiss. There are, in the end, two miserably wrong responses to the repeated collapse of every hope. It is wrong, of course, to go on believing that next time will be different. But it is also wrong to believe that, because the next time will not be different, the current situation is one of pure chaos without structure, without possibilities or potentialities. It is wrong to fantasize, starry-eyed, that something is coming in order, effortlessly, to solve all problems; but it is also wrong to pretend, hollow-eyed, that it only remains to give oneself to pragmatic efforts at ensuring endurable survival.

What fires descend onto what rocks before us today, in whose dancing flames we might, with enough care and enough study, begin to recognize the latent potency of our own situation? What book descends from heaven today that, once we have been bidden to read it, fills us with prophetic insight enough to see the fullness rather than the emptiness of the world? What preaching ought we today to pursue—if, that is, we still have the courage to hope to scandalize our own contemporaries by insisting that the messianic remains relevant? And, then, what wilderness should we be prepared to flee to?

Tender Mercies in English Scriptural Idiom and in Nephi's Record

Miranda Wilcox

NEPHI RECORDS DIVINE BEINGS inviting humans to participate in the sacred story of salvation and humans petitioning divine beings for aid in their mortal affliction. The first chapter of Nephi's story introduces linguistic, textual, and narrative questions about how humans should engage with and produce holy books that memorialize these divine-human relations in heaven and on earth. For Nephi, a central element of these relationships is "tender mercies" (1 Nephi 1:20). What are tender mercies? How do the Lord's tender mercies make the chosen faithful "mighty, even unto the power of deliverance"?

Nephi's striking phrase has become popular in Latter-day Saint discourse since Elder David A. Bednar preached of the "tender mercies of the Lord" at general conference in April 2005. He defined *tender mercies* as "very personal and individualized blessings, strength, protection, assurances, guidance, loving-kindnesses, consolation, support, and spiritual gifts which we receive from and because of and through the Lord Jesus Christ."[1] I would like to extend this discussion and reconsider this definition with respect to Nephi's record by exploring the biblical sources and the transmission of this beloved phrase through English scriptural idiom.

---

1. David A. Bednar, "The Tender Mercies of the Lord," *Ensign*, May 2005, 99.

Nephi explains that he has acquired "a great knowledge of the goodness and the mysteries of God" and that he will share this knowledge in his record (1 Nephi 1:1). To make this record, Nephi must translate his personal experience and spiritual knowledge into the medium of written language, a medium circumscribed by its lexical resources and cultural traditions. Nephi acknowledges his record's linguistic and cultural hybridity in blending ancestral Jewish traditions with imperial Egyptian script: "Yea, I make a record in the language of my father, which consists of the learning of the Jews and the language of the Egyptians. And I know that the record which I make to be true. And I make it with mine own hand, and I make it according to my knowledge" (1 Nephi 1:2–3). As modern readers, we are limited in our ability to perceive and evaluate these linguistic and cultural contours because we lack access to the original language of Nephi's record. Instead, we have Joseph Smith's English translation, a translation made in the language of Smith's own ancestors. Like Nephi's Reformed Egyptian, Joseph's English is encoded with linguistic and cultural hybridity, but unlike Nephi's language, the history of the English language has been well documented. Consequently, we must triangulate the meaning of Nephi's phrase *tender mercies* through the lens of Joseph's translation, which is itself embedded in a long tradition of fashioning English as a functional and resonant medium for scripture.

The rich history of translating scriptural texts into English involves generations of effort by many, including Ælfric, John Wyclif, William Tyndale, English expatriates in Geneva, and King James's scholars. The translators of each generation were challenged to recapture the ancient scriptural truths anew in the common language of their day. As an inheritor of this tradition, Joseph Smith likewise recasts Nephi's sixth-century Jewish world using the linguistic resources of the scriptural idiom popular in early nineteenth-century Protestant America—that is, the language of the King James Bible. Before we can understand tender mercies with respect to Nephi's "learning of [his] father," we need to explore the history of the term in the learning of Joseph's fathers.

The learning of Joseph's fathers: Mercy in the Hebrew Bible and in English scriptural idiom

The phrase *tender mercies* did not originate in the Book of Mormon.[2] It appears eleven times in the King James Bible:[3] ten times in the Psalms and once in Proverbs, where it consistently renders the Hebrew word *raḥămîm*, an intensive, plural, nominal form of the verb *rāḥam*, meaning to "love deeply, have mercy, be compassionate."[4] *Raḥămîm* appears thirty-nine times in the Hebrew Bible (eleven times in the Psalms),[5] in contexts articulating God's intrinsic and steadfast love and his patient willingness to forgive in order to preserve relation with both the obedient and the unfaithful. The cluster of occurrences of the phrase *tender mercies* and the term *raḥămîm* in the Psalms indicates a close relationship between this term and the language of Israel's songs of praise and lament.

In the Hebrew Bible, the stem *rḥm* and its cognates refer to an intense visceral love and intimate commitment rooted in a natural bond of kinship and creation, especially of a mother for her child (for example, 1 Kings 3:26 and Isaiah 49:15) and of God for his children (for example, Isaiah 63:7, 15; Psalm 145:9).[6] *Rāḥam* is linked with a homophone, *reḥem* ("womb"), and this verbal relation anchors the emotion of *rḥm* in physiological pain felt deeply in one's inner organs while observing another's vulnerability: a mother for her baby dependent on her care, and God for his creatures susceptible to sin and

---

2. The phrase *tender mercies* appears in 1 Nephi 1:20; 8:8; and Ether 6:12.

3. See Psalms 25:6; 40:11; 51:1; 69:16; 77:9; 79:8; 103:4; 119:77, 156; 145:9; and Proverbs 12:10. *Tender mercy* appears twice in the New Testament: Luke 1:78 and James 5:11.

4. *Theological Wordbook of the Old Testament*, ed. R. Laird Harris, Gleason L. Archer Jr., and Bruce K. Waltke (Chicago: Moody Press, 1980), s.v. "rāḥam," 2:841. For a thorough analysis, see *Theological Dictionary of the Old Testament*, ed. G. Johannes Botterweck, Helmer Ringgren, and Heinz-Josef Fabry, trans. David E. Green (Grand Rapids, MI: Eerdmans, 1974–2004), s.v. "רחם *rḥm*," 13:437–54.

5. The Hebrew word *raḥămîm* occurs eleven times in the Masoretic text of the Psalms, including the previously listed instances in note 3 plus one in Psalm 106:46 (KJV 106:45).

6. See *Theological Dictionary*, ed. Botterweck et al., 13:438–43.

suffering. Such pain compels a compassionate and merciful response that alleviates this suffering.

In the Hebrew Bible, *rhm* primarily refers to a fundamental and enduring attribute of Yahweh, and it is "an essential constituent of the relationship between God and humanity."[7] For example, in Exodus 34:6, Yahweh proclaims himself to Moses on Mount Sinai: "The Lord, the Lord, a God merciful (*raḥûm*) and gracious (*hannûn*), slow to anger, and abounding in steadfast love (*ḥesed*) and faithfulness (*'ĕmet*)."[8] The same constellation of words appears in Psalm 25, where the psalmist expresses powerful confidence in Yahweh's love and mercy amid petitions for divine rescue, teaching, and forgiveness.[9] Walter Brueggemann notes that this psalm juxtaposes themes of divine fidelity and human failure and in doing so models candid acknowledgment of human vulnerability, for "the candor of suffering ... moves to a gratitude rooted in confidence that God's *ḥesed* will prevail. Candor turns to gratitude, suffering turns to hope, lament turns to praise."[10]

> 6. Be mindful of your mercy (*raḥămîm*), O Lord, and of your steadfast love (*ḥĕsādîm*),
> > for they have been from old.
> 7. Do not remember the sins of my youth or my transgressions;
> > according to your steadfast love (*ḥesed*) remember me,
> > for your goodness' sake, Lord!

---

7. *Theological Dictionary*, ed. Botterweck et al., 13:441.

8. Katharine D. Sakenfeld, *The Meaning of* Hesed *in the Hebrew Bible: A New Inquiry* (Missoula, MT: Scholars Press, 1978), 112–22. These verses have been interpreted as the heart of the Sinai covenant and are used liturgically in Judaism; see echoes in Psalms 86:15; 103:8; and 145:8.

9. John Goldingay, *Psalms: Vol. 1, Psalms 1–41* (Grand Rapids, MI: Baker Academic, 2006), 368. See also Walter Brueggemann and William H. Bellinger Jr., *Psalms*, New Cambridge Bible Commentary (Cambridge: Cambridge University Press, 2014), 130–33. Goldingay suggests that the acrostic form of Psalm 25 may have been "designed as a model prayer" (368).

10. Walter Brueggemann, *The Psalms and the Life of Faith*, ed. Patrick D. Miller (Minneapolis: Fortress Press, 1995), 199–200.

8. Good and upright is the Lord;
   therefore he instructs the sinners in the way.
9. He leads the humble in what is right,
   and teaches the humble his way.
10. All the paths of the Lord are steadfast love (*ḥesed*) and
    faithfulness (*'ĕmet*),
      for those who keep his covenant and his
      testimonies.[11]

In verse 6, *raḥămîm* is paired with *ḥesed*, a word referring to an "act
that preserves or promotes life," constituted by mutual and enduring
"goodness, grace, kindness."[12] This frequent pairing can be treated
as "a compound of complementary expressions: *ḥesed* expresses the
fundamental goodness of God, *rḥm* the special favor shown by God
in the face of a situation of sin and affliction."[13] Like *raḥămîm*, *ḥesed*
is a rich and flexible word of relation. Scholars have considered *ḥesed*
as "loyal kindness," the reciprocity of mutual beneficence between
two parties who have entered a relationship entailing responsibility
to the other party. While some scholars describe *ḥesed* as involving
a formal covenant, others stress that this commitment is rooted in
moral responsibility rather than legal obligation.[14] The mutuality in
this relation involves reciprocal actions: a person "who receives an
act of *ḥesed* responds with a similar act of *ḥesed*," or at least a person
"who demonstrates *ḥesed* is justified in expecting an equivalent act in
return."[15] When referring to divine action, Katharine Sakenfeld concludes that "*ḥesed* was a particularly useful word for speaking of God's
relationship to his people, collectively and individually, because it held
together in a single expression an emphasis on divine freedom on the

---

11. Translation by Brueggemann, *Psalms and the Life of Faith*, 198; see also Brueggemann and Bellinger, *Psalms*, 130–31.

12. *Theological Dictionary*, ed. Botterweck et al., s.v. "ḥesed," 5:51–52.

13. *Theological Dictionary*, ed. Botterweck et al., 13:452.

14. For example, see Nelson Glueck, *Hesed in the Bible*, trans. Alfred Gottschalk
(Cincinnati: Hebrew Union College Press, 1967), and Harold M. Kamsler, "Hesed—
Mercy or Loyalty?" *Jewish Bible Quarterly* 27/3 (1999): 183–85.

15. *Theological Dictionary*, ed. Botterweck et al., 5:47.

one hand and divine commitment on the other, the emphasis on divine power ... and divine care ... an emphasis on human need and weakness ... and human responsibility to trust in God alone."[16] Dan Belnap highlights the agent reciprocation involved in acts of *ḥesed,* and he emphasizes that humans reciprocate physical or spiritual deliverance of divine *ḥesed* by obedience to God and by performing acts of *ḥesed* on behalf of others, "since we cannot truly reciprocate in kind to God."[17]

Ḥesed is repeated in verses 7 and 10 of Psalm 25, where it is linked to God's faithfulness (*'ĕmet*). Scholars consider the pairing of *ḥesed* and *'ĕmet* to be a hendiadys in which one noun serves to describe the other; thus, the pair of words could mean "faithful love" or "steadfast kindness."[18] In his study of the collocations with *ḥesed,* Gordon R. Clark concludes that this collocation emphasizes the fidelity, faithfulness, trustworthiness, and steadfastness that characterize the agents' interaction and the "permanence, certainty, and lasting validity of the demonstration or promise of *ḥesed*."[19] This triad of terms— *raḥămîm, ḥesed,* and *'ĕmet* —deepen the relational aspects of mercy in ancient Israel's songs of worship.[20] The subtle variations among these complementary and overlapping terms praise God's multifaceted and constant nature.

To explore how much of the Israelite theology of mercy embedded in the word *raḥămîm* and its related words was conveyed in translations made through the centuries, I will trace how the verse Psalm 25:6 has been rendered through the development of English scriptural idiom. This case study illustrates how scripture is circumscribed by the medium of the language in which it is rendered. The visceral and reciprocal nature of *raḥămîm* was effaced in Greek, Latin, Old and Middle

---

16. Sakenfeld, *Meaning of Hesed,* 149.

17. Dan Belnap, "'How Excellent Is Thy Lovingkindness': The Gospel Principle of *Hesed,*" in *The Gospel of Jesus Christ in the Old Testament,* ed. D. Kelly Ogden, Jared W. Ludlow, and Kerry Muhlestein, 38th Annual Sidney Sperry Symposium (Provo, UT: BYU Religious Studies Center and Deseret Book, 2009), 182.

18. *Theological Wordbook,* s.v. "חסד ḥsd," 1:305–7.

19. Gordon R. Clark, *The Word* Hesed *in the Hebrew Bible* (Sheffield: JSOT Press, 1993), 267.

20. See also Lamentations 3:22–23 and Psalm 89:24, 33.

English translations and was somewhat recovered in Early Modern English translations during the sixteenth century.

The story of the transmission and translation of Psalm 25 begins with the compilation of the Hebrew book of Psalms during the Second Temple period. The authorship and date of the composition of Psalm 25 is unknown, as is the case with most of the psalms. Many biblical scholars believe that ancient Israel composed prayers and songs for use in preexilic communal and family worship, including in temple liturgy and in prayer rituals, and continued to do so during the Babylonian exile. Priests and scribes collected these prayers and songs during the postexilic period, and the collection eventually became canonized as the book of Psalms.[21] The Hebrew Masoretic text of Psalm 25:6 reads:[22]

זְכֹר־רַחֲמֶיךָ יְהוָה וַחֲסָדֶיךָ כִּי מֵעוֹלָם הֵמָּה:

Modern translations of the Hebrew Bible typically render *raḥămîm* as "compassion" and *ḥesed* as "mercy" or "great commitment."[23] As discussed above, *raḥămîm* and *ḥesed* are not synonyms. Rather, *raḥămîm* is the physiological and emotional response to the suffering of a loved one, and this compassionate emotion generates the merciful action of *ḥesed* on the loved one's behalf.

In the second and third centuries BC, Greek translations were made of Hebrew scriptures for Hellenized Jews, especially those living in Egypt. Greek was the common language of the Mediterranean world for several centuries, and these translations made the Hebrew

---

21. Goldingay, *Psalms*, 35–37, see also 24–32. Goldingay summarizes: "[The Psalter] is known in approximately the form we have it to the authors of the LXX (in Alexandria in the third or second, century BC?) and to the Qumran community (a little later), and there are no indications of Greek influence on the Psalms. All this implies that the Psalter came into being in something like the form we know it sometime in the Second Temple period, in Persian or early Greek times. From the beginning it was presumably among the authoritative resources of the Jewish community, and in this sense the time it came into being is also the time when it became canonical" (35).

22. *JPS Hebrew-English Tanakh*, 2nd ed. (Philadelphia: Jewish Publication Society, 1999), 1439.

23. Goldingay, *Psalms*, 365.

scriptures widely available. The best-known Greek translation was the Septuagint, in which Psalm 25:6 is rendered:

μνήσθητι τῶν οἰκτιρμῶν σου κύριε, καὶ τὰ ἐλέη σου, ὅτι ἀπὸ τοῦ αἰῶνός εἰσιν.[24]

Oiktirmós translates *raḥămîm*, and *eleos* translates *ḥesed*. In this verse, the translators of the Septuagint used two of three words that expressed mercy and compassion in the Greek lexicon: "*eleos* refers to the feeling of pity, *oiktirmós*, and especially its root *oiktos*, to the exclamation of pity at the sight of another's ill-fortune." However, they did not use *splanchna*, the word used to refer "to the seat of emotions, the inward parts or what today would be called the heart," which may have preserved the visceral connotations of *raḥămîm*.[25] As in any translation, the entire semantic range and complex nuances of the source language cannot be fully captured in the target language, so a translator looks for comparable, compatible, or parallel linguistic concepts in the target language. Mercy was not valued the same way in the Hellenistic worldview as in the Semitic, so it is not surprising that the constellation of Greek words for mercy did not align exactly with the Hebrew words.

Pity was not always a desirable emotion in Greek culture. Aristotle defines *eleos* in *Rhetoric* 2.8 as "a kind of pain in the case of an apparent destructive or painful harm in one not deserving to encounter it," a misfortune that "one might expect oneself, or one's own, to suffer."[26] According to David Konstan, an expert on ancient emotions, "Greek pity [*eleos/oiktos*] was not an instinctive response to another person's pain, but depended on a judgment of whether the other's suffering

24. *The Septuagint with Apocrypha: Greek and English*, ed. Sir Lancelot C. L. Brenton (Grand Rapids, MI: Zondervan, 1980), 711.

25. *The New International Dictionary of New Testament Theology*, ed. Colin Brown (Exeter: Paternoster Press, 1976), s.v. "Mercy, Compassion." See also *Theological Dictionary of the New Testament*, ed. Gerhard Kittel, Gerhard Friedrich, and Geoffrey William Bromiley (Grand Rapids, MI: Eerdmans, 1964), 1:680.

26. Quoted in David Konstan, *The Emotions of the Ancient Greeks: Studies in Aristotle and Classical Literature* (Toronto: University of Toronto Press, 2006), 204. See Aristotle, *Rhetoric* 1385b13–16.

was deserved or not."[27] The Stoics, who were writing during the same period as the Septuagint translation was being produced, considered pity to be a pathological emotion to be avoided. In Greek discourse, the psychological and judicial elements of these terms were emphasized, in contrast to the physiological and social dimensions of the Hebrew terms.

During the second and third centuries AD, multiple Latin translations of the Septuagint circulated in Christian communities in the Roman Empire. Around 380, Pope Damasus commissioned Jerome to revise these various Latin translations of the Greek New Testament; after Jerome completed the New Testament, he turned his attention to translating the Old Testament. During the 380s and 390s, Jerome produced three revisions and one translation of the Psalms.[28] Although Jerome consulted sources in multiple languages, he selected Latin words that lessened the distinction between *raḥămîm* and *ḥesed*. First, he revised the second-century Old Latin version from Africa, and he consulted Greek versions in his second revision, the *Psalterium Romanum*. Then he consulted Origin's Hexapla for his third revision, the *Psalterium Gallicanum*; this version was transmitted in the Vulgate and used in medieval liturgy for over a millennium. While living in Bethlehem, he produced a new Latin translation of the Hebrew psalms called the *Psalterium Hebraicum*. There are minor variations among Jerome's different versions of Psalm 25:6.

> [Romanum] Reminiscere miserationum tuarum domine et misericordia tua quae a saeculo sunt.

> [Gallican] Reminiscere miserationum tuarum domine et misericordiarum tuarum quae a seculo sunt.

> [Hebraicum] Reminiscere miserationum tuarum domine atque misericordiarum tuarum: quod a seclo sunt.

> [Remember your mercies Lord and your mercy-heartednesses which are from the beginning.]

---

27. Konstan, *Emotions of the Ancient Greeks*, 201.

28. Susan Gillingham, *Psalms through the Centuries: Volume 1* (Oxford: Wiley-Blackwell, 2008), 36–37.

Jerome consistently uses the plural genitive of *miseratio*, "pity, compassion," for *raḥămîm/oiktirmós* and in the two later versions the plural genitive of *misericordia*, "mercy, compassion," or literally "mercy-heartedness" for *ḥesed/eleos*.[29] Jerome seems to have interpreted *raḥămîm* and *ḥesed* as synonyms and does not utilize the potential parallel between the visceral connotations implicit in the compound *misericordia* and those of *raḥămîm*.

Miseratio and *misericordia* were often used synonymously in Christian Latin discourse and conveyed a new ethics of relation outlined in the beatitude in Matthew 5:7: "Beati misericordes quia ipsi misericordiam consequentur" [Blessed are the merciful: for they shall obtain mercy]. This Christian ethical orientation contrasted with the Stoic view expressed by Seneca, in which *misericordia* was a "weakness of souls" that good men should avoid, "for it is the falling of a weak nature that succumbs to the sight of other's ills."[30] In the early seventh century, Isidore of Seville provided an etymological explanation that again highlighted the visceral relation between misery and compassion: "The term 'pitying' (*misericors*) is assigned from one's having compassion for another's distress (*miseria*), and from this pity (*misericordia*) is so called, because it makes miserable (*miserum*) the heart (*cor*) of one who grieves over the distress of another. However, this etymology does not apply in every case, because in God there is *misericordia* without any 'misery of heart.'"[31] Latin Christian discourse shifted the locus of

29. Charlton T. Lewis and Charles Short, *A Latin Dictionary* (Oxford: Oxford University Press, 2002), s.v. "Misericordia."

30. Seneca, *De Clementia* 2.6.4, "vitium est animorum"; 2.5.1, "Est enim vitium pusilli animi ad speciem alienorum malorum succidentis." See Cilliers Breytenbach, *Grace, Reconciliation, Concord: The Death of Christ in Graeco-Roman Metaphors* (Leiden: Brill, 2010), 232–33; and Sarah Byers, "The Psychology of Compassion: Stoicism in *City of God* 9.5," in *Augustine's City of God: A Critical Guide*, ed. James Wetzel (Cambridge: Cambridge University Press, 2012), 130–39.

31. Isidore, *Etymologiae* 10.164, in *Isidori hispalensis episcopi etymolgiarum sive originvm*, ed. W. M. Lindsay, 2 vols. (Oxford: Clarendon Press, 1911), "Misericors a con-patiendo alienae miseriae vocabulum est sortius: et hinc appellate misericordia, quod miserum cor faciat dolentis aliena miseria. Non autem occurrit ubique haec etymologia; nam est in Deo misericordia sine ulla cordis miseria." Stephen A. Barney, W. J. Lewis, J. A. Beach, and Oliver Berghof, trans., *The "Etymologies" of Isidore of Seville* (Cambridge:

compassion back to the physiological and social, though it excluded God from participating in emotional mutuality with humans.

The history of English scriptural idiom begins with the conversion of the Anglo-Saxon kingdoms in the sixth and seventh centuries. The Anglo-Saxons spoke a West Germanic language we now call Old English and could not understand the Latin Bibles brought by Christian missionaries from Ireland, Gaul, and Italy. Eventually a small percentage of Anglo-Saxons joined monasteries and learned Latin, but the majority of Anglo-Saxons would have had to rely on vernacular summaries, paraphrases, illustrations, and translations of the Bible to learn about the Christian faith.

The oldest extant translation of a biblical text into Old English is the interlinear gloss added in the mid-ninth century to the Psalterium Romanum in the mid-eighth-century manuscript London, British Library, Cotton Vespasian A.i (usually called the Vespasian Psalter). It is not surprising that a vernacular version of the Psalms was needed. Reciting the Psalms was the foundation of the monastic liturgy and an integral part of the monastic curriculum. Over the course of a week, monks and nuns recited the entire Psalter.[32] The Old English gloss for Psalm 25:6 was rendered by the glossator of the Vespasian Psalter as:

> Gemyne <u>mildsa</u> ðinra dryhten & <u>mildheortnis</u> ðin ða from werulde sind.[33]
>
> [Be mindful of thy mercies Lord and thy mercy-heartedness which are from the beginning of the world.][34]

Cambridge University Press, 2006), 223. See also Leslie Lockett, *Anglo-Saxon Psychologies in the Vernacular and Latin Traditions* (Toronto: University of Toronto, 2011), 211.

32. For a comprehensive analysis of the use of the Psalms in Anglo-Saxon England, see M. J. Toswell, *The Anglo-Saxon Psalter* (Turnhout: Brepols, 2014). See also George H. Brown, "The Psalms as the Foundation of Anglo-Saxon Learning," in *The Place of the Psalms in the Intellectual Culture of the Middle Ages*, ed. Nancy van Deusen (Albany: State University of New York Press, 1999), 1–24.

33. Sherman M. Kuhn, ed., *The Vespasian Psalter* (Ann Arbor: University of Michigan Press, 1965).

34. The Old English gloss "worlde" [world] for "saeculo" [time, world] literally renders the Latin idiom "a saeculo" [in the beginning].

The Old English gloss provides a straightforward translation of the Latin psalm. Although the Old English word *milds* became the modern English word *mild*, in early Germanic languages it and its cognates meant "mercy, pity, and compassion." The compound *mildheortness* is a calque (or a loan translation) of *misericordia* in which the Latin components are rendered in the same pattern with Old English lexical correspondence. Anglo-Saxons continued glossing and translating the Psalms over the next two hundred years; fourteen psalter manuscripts with vernacular glosses survive from the tenth and eleventh centuries.[35] The subsequent psalter glosses consistently employed the vocabulary of the Vespasian gloss. Anglo-Saxons also produced independent translations of psalms. The Paris Psalter contains Old English prose paraphrases of Psalms 1–50 and Paris, Bibliothèque nationale de France, MS Fonds latin 8824, a manuscript that dates from perhaps the mid-eleventh century, contains Old English metrical versions of Psalms 51–150.[36] The prose paraphrase renders the words from the psalter glosses of Psalm 25:6 in more fluid Old English syntax.

> Gemun, Drihten, þinra <u>miltsunga</u> and þinre <u>mildheort-</u>
> <u>nesse</u> þe fram fruman worlde wæs.[37]
>
> [Be mindful, Lord, of thy mercies and of thy mercy-heartedness which was from the beginning of the world.]

Following the example of the Latin Vulgate, the doubling of *mild-* in Old English translations perpetuates the loss of distinction between the Hebrew terms *raḥămîm* and *ḥesed*, of which Anglo-Saxons had no direct knowledge.

After the Norman Conquest in 1066, the influx of French-speaking aristocrats and ecclesiastical leaders displaced Old English as a literary language. Over several hundred years, a hybrid language called Middle

---

35. Phillip Pulsiano, ed., *Old English Glossed Psalters: Psalms 1–50* (Toronto: University of Toronto, 2001).

36. King Alfred (849–899) has traditionally been credited as the composer of the prose paraphrases of the first fifty psalms; however, his authorship has been disputed.

37. Patrick P. O'Neill, ed., *King Alfred's Old English Prose Translation of the First Fifty Psalms* (Cambridge, MA: Medieval Academy of America, 2001), 126.

English emerged from Germanic and Scandinavian roots and exposure to French. Middle English can be characterized by a simplified inflectional system and by an enriched vocabulary; this fluidity offered new possibilities for biblical translation.[38] In addition, a growing focus on individual piety in the thirteenth century stimulated the production of the Books of Hours, which encouraged laity to emulate in their private devotional life the clerical practice of daily reciting psalms.[39]

Multiple Middle English translations of Latin psalms were made from the mid-1200s to 1400. These translations were made in several Middle English dialects, and they employed words with Old English antecedents and more recent loan words. The Surtees Psalter, a Middle English metrical paraphrase, was composed between circa 1250 and 1300. Psalm 25:6 is rendered in the following couplet:

> Lauerd, ofe þine <u>reuthes</u> mine þou mare,
> And of þine <u>milþes</u>, of werld þat are.[40]

> [Lord, be thou more mindful of thy pities, and of thy mercies, that are from the world.]

This northern dialect employs *reuth*, a word from Old Norse meaning "pity, compassion, and sympathy," and *milthe*, a word from the Old English *milds*, "mercy."[41] Dating from the mid-fourteenth century, the West Midlands Psalter provides a Middle English prose translation of Psalm 25:6:

---

38. Richard Marsden, "The Bible in English in the Middle Ages," in *The Practice of the Bible in the Middle Ages: Production, Reception, and Performance in Western Christianity*, ed. Susan Boynton and Diane J. Reilly (New York: Columbia University Press, 2011), 272–95, and "'In the twinkling of an eye': The English Scripture before Tyndale," *Leeds Studies in English*, n.s., 31 (2000): 145–72.

39. Eamon Duffy, *Marking the Hours: English People and Their Prayers 1240–1570* (New Haven: Yale University Press, 2006).

40. Joseph Stevenson, ed., *Anglo-Saxon and Early English Psalter*, Surtees Society Publications 16 and 19 (London, 1843–47), 156. See also James H. Morey, *Book and Verse: A Guide to Middle English Biblical Literature* (Urbana: University of Illinois Press, 2000), 174–75.

41. *Middle English Dictionary*, Middle English Compendium, University of Michigan, s.v. "reuth(e (n.)," and "milthe (n. & adj.)."

By-þenche þe, Lord, of þy <u>pites</u> and of þy <u>mercies</u> þat ben of þe world.[42]

[Be thoughtful, Lord, of thy pities and of thy mercies that be from the world.]

This West Midlands dialect employs two Old French loanwords: *pité* and *merci*, both of which are still used in similar semantic ranges in Modern English.

In circa 1340, the mystic hermit Richard Rolle of Hampole (1290–1349) produced his *English Psalter*, which included a translation and commentary for his friend Margaret Kirkby, who later became an anchoress. Rolle emphasized that his translation could be used for devotional purposes by persons who did not know Latin, for psalms provided "a moral yet mystical bridge between the physical world of words and heavenly realities."[43] Rolle rendered Psalm 25:6 with commentary:

Vmthynke ye of thi mercyingis lord; and of thi mercys, the whilke ere fra the warld.[44]

[Remember thy merciful works Lord, and thy mercies, those which are from the beginning of the world.]

Rolle uses *mercy* to signify both an emotional response to another's suffering and the action prompted by this feeling. Rolle's psalter was popular in southern England and much copied and revised by Lollards

42. Karl D. Bülbring, ed., *The Earliest Complete Prose Psalter,* Early English Text Society 97 (London, 1891), 27. See also Morey, *Book and Verse,* 175.

43. Gillingham, *Psalms through the Ages,* 124; Morey, *Book and Verse,* 175–77; David Daniell, *The Bible in English: Its History and Influence* (New Haven: Yale University Press, 2003), 101–2.

44. Richard Rolle, *The Psalter, or Psalms of David and Certain Canticles, with a Translation and Exposition in English by Richard Rolle of Hampole,* ed. H. R. Bramley (Oxford: Clarendon Press, 1884), 88. Rolle's commentary on this verse: "Vmthynk the, for men wenes thou has forgetyn, for thou gifes noght alstite as thai wild, of thi mercyingis, that is, of the werkis of thi mercy: and of thi mercys, the whilke ere kindly in the, and thai ere fra the beginynge of the warld: for neyer was thou wthouten mercy."

who advocated for ecclesiastical reform and for vernacular translation of the Bible in the fourteenth and fifteenth centuries.[45]

In the 1370s and 1380s amid "profound clerical anxieties about lay access to the Bible," manuscripts containing Middle English translations of the entire Latin Vulgate began circulating in England.[46] These manuscripts were associated with John Wyclif, a prominent scholar at Oxford, and his friends; however, the names of the translators remain unknown. The translation of the Wycliffite Bibles was likely a corporate enterprise in multiple stages.[47] The first phase of translation produced "a closely literal" rendering of the Latin Bible, and the second phase "a more idiomatic revision."[48] This sequence of revision is evident in Psalm 25:6.

> Earlier Version: Recorde of thi <u>mercy deedis</u>, Lord; and of thi <u>mercies</u> that fro the world ben.
>
> [Remember your merciful deeds, Lord, and your mercies that have been from the beginning of the world.]
>
> Later Version: Lord, haue thou mynde of thi <u>merciful doyngis</u>; and of thi <u>mercies</u> that ben fro the world.
>
> [Lord, be mindful of your merciful actions, and of your mercies that have been from the beginning of the world.]

Wycliffite Bibles circulated secretly for the next 150 years in spite of intense repression after ecclesiastical legislation in 1407–9 prohibited "the use of any recent, unlicensed translation." Approximately 230 manuscripts survived, more than any other Middle English text.[49]

In both versions of the Wycliffite Bible and in Rolle's Psalter, the French loanword *merci* replaced the native Old English word *milds*. The root of the Old French *merci* was "Latin *merces* [which] meant

---

45. Gillingham, *Psalms through the Ages*, 124.

46. Mary Dove, *The First English Bible: The Text and Context of the Wycliffite Versions* (Cambridge: Cambridge University Press, 2007), 10.

47. Dove, *First English Bible*, 68–82.

48. Dove, *First English Bible*, 3; for more details, see 137–88. See also Daniell, *Bible in English*, 76–85.

49. Dove, *First English Bible*, 1 and 35–67; Daniell, *Bible in English*, 67.

'payment, reward.' In the Christian era the [commercial] notion of a 'reward' was taken up and reapplied metaphorically to the 'compassion given freely by God to humankind,' and the word passed into Old French (in the form of *merci*) with the broader sense 'compassion,' and hence 'forbearance from punishment.'"[50] *Merci* appears in the Middle English corpus as early as the beginning of the thirteenth century, and its semantic range encompasses social responses of pardon, clemency, and forgiveness; emotional responses of pity, compassion, and favor; and theological concepts of divine atonement, propitiation, and grace.[51]

By the early sixteenth century, humanistic renewal of interest in Hebrew and Greek in Western Europe revealed inconsistencies and divergences in the Latin Vulgate, which spurred scholars to call for new translations from original sources. Simultaneously, the spread of the evangelical doctrine that all Christians should have access to the word of God in their own tongue increased the intensity of vernacular scriptural translation and publication.[52] However, translating the Bible in England was politically dangerous and divisive. Henry VIII and his advisors considered vernacular translations of the Bible to be seditious because they undermined the authority and power of the king and the Catholic Church. Until Henry's break with Rome in the 1530s, translations of the Bible into English were prohibited.[53] Nevertheless, there was a proliferation of English translations of psalms during the sixteenth century as scholars began referring to Hebrew, Greek, and contemporary vernacular versions. The first group of translators

---

50. John Ayto, *Word Origins*, 2nd ed. (London: A & C Black, 2005), s.v. "mercy"; *Webster's Word Histories* (Springfield, MA: Merriam-Webster, 1989), 304; and the *Oxford English Dictionary*, s.v. "mercy."

51. *Middle English Dictionary*, s.v. "merci."

52. George R. Potter, "Zwingli and the Book of Psalms," *The Sixteenth Century Journal* 10/2 (1979): 42–50; Gerald Hobbs, "Martin Bucer and the Englishing of the Psalms: Pseudonymity in the Service of Early English Protestant Piety," in *Martin Bucer: Reforming Church and Community*, ed. D. F. Wright (Cambridge: Cambridge University Press, 1994), 161–75.

53. Richard Duerden, "Equivalence or Power? Authority and Reformation Biblical Translation," in *The Bible as Book: The Reformation*, ed. Orlaith O'Sullivan (London: Oak Knoll Press, 2000), 9–23.

comprised English scholars living on the continent in exile because of their evangelical sympathies.

George Joye published the first sixteenth-century English translation of the Psalms in 1530 as *The Psalter of David in Englyshe* in Antwerp. Joye's colloquial psalm translations were also published in England in the form of a primer, a devotional manual and school text for the laity.[54] Joye's source was *Psalmorum libri quinque ad ebraicam veritatem versi* by reformer Martin Bucer of Strasbourg. Bucer translated the Hebrew of Psalm 25:6 as: "Memor sis <u>misericordiae</u> tuae Autophyes, & <u>benignitatis</u> tuae, quando quidem iis praestas ab initio,"[55] which Joye rendered into colloquial English as:

> Lorde remember thy <u>mercy</u> and thy <u>gracious favoure</u>: for in theis thynges thou excellest even from the beginnynge.[56]

Joye followed Bucer's somewhat freer translation, whose periphrastic rendering prioritized plain sense over literal verbal correspondence. Unlike many of the Latin, Old English, and Middle English psalm translations, Bucer's and Joye's translations distinguish between the Hebrew words *raḥămîm* and *ḥesed*, and this verbal distinction set a precedent for subsequent English psalm translations. Bucer also aligns *raḥămîm* with the more apt Latin term *misericordia*.

Four years later, another English expatriate in Antwerp, Miles Coverdale, produced a paraphrase of Jan van Campen's Latin translation of

54. Hobbs, "Bucer and the Englishing of the Psalms," 163–64; Rivkah Zim, *English Metrical Psalms: Poetry as Praise and Prayer, 1535–1601* (Cambridge: Cambridge University Press, 1987), 31–33.

55. Martin Bucer, *Psalmorum libri quinque ad Ebraicam veritatem versi et familiari explanatione elucidate per Aretium Felinum* (Strasbourg: G. Ulricher, 1529), 139. Digitized by Bayerische StaatsBibliothek digital.

56. George Joye, *The Psalter of Dauid in Englishe purely a[n]d faithfully tra[n]slated aftir the texte of Feline* ([Antwerp: Merten de Keyser], 1530), fol. 36r, STC 2nd ed./2370, *EEBO*. Four years later, Joye translated Ulrich Zwingli's Latin and German version into English as *Davids Psalter*: "Remember thy mercy and goodnes: which thou of euer vsetè" (25:6). George Joye, *Dauids Psalter, diligently and faithfully tra[n]slated by George Ioye, with breif arguments before euery Psalme, declaringe the effecte therof* ([Antwerp: Merten de Keyser], 1534), STC 2nd ed./2372, *EEBO*.

the Hebrew psalms. Coverdale rendered Campen's version of Psalm 25:6, "Reuoca in memoriam Domine <u>clementiam</u> & <u>benignitatem</u> tuam, quibus seculis superioribus tam liberaliter usus es erga tuos," as:

> Call to remembraunce Lorde thy <u>kyndnesse</u> & <u>gentyl-
nesse</u>, whyche in fore tymes thou hast used so liberally
towarde those that are thyne.[57]

Coverdale faithfully renders Campen's Latin in 1534, but he makes considerable changes to this verse when he publishes his translation of the Psalms in the first edition of the entire English Bible the following year.

> Call to remembraunce, O LORDE, thy <u>tender mercyes</u> &
thy <u>louinge kyndnesses</u>, which haue bene euer of olde.[58]

David Daniell and Gordon Campbell credit Coverdale with coining the term *tender mercies* in his translation of Psalm 25:6: "Coverdale had an excellent ear, and many of his fine phrases have resonated down the centuries, transmitted by the KJV. His magnificent rendering of Psalm 25:6 … brought the word 'loving kindness' and the phrase 'tender mercies' into English and into the mainstream of biblical translations."[59] The use of plural *mercies* renders the plural *raḥămîm*,

---

57. Miles Coverdale, *A paraphrasis vpon all the Psalmes of Dauid, made by Iohannes Campensis, reader of the Hebrue lecture in the vniuersite of Louane, and translated out of Latine into Englysshe* (1539), STC 2nd ed./2372.6, EEBO.

58. Miles Coverdale, trans., *Biblia the Byble, that is, the holy Scrypture of the Olde and New Testament, faithfully translated in to Englyshe* (1535), STC 2nd ed./2063, EEBO.

59. Gordon Campbell, *Bible: The Story of the King James Version, 1611–2011* (Oxford: Oxford University Press, 2010), 16. Daniell makes a similar claim in *The Bible in English*, 181. Although Coverdale may have been the first to use the phrase *tender mercy* in a psalm translation, he did not coin the phrase. In his translation of the New Testament published in 1534, William Tyndale employs *tender mercy* to translate "splanchna eleous" in Luke 1:78 and "splanchna oiktirmou" in Colossians 3:12. In his influential Latin translation of the New Testament first published in 1516, Desiderius Erasmus renders the Greek Septuagint as "viscera misericordiae" in Luke 1:78 and "viscera miserationum" in Colossians 3:12.

and the adjective *tender* communicates the intensified form of the Hebrew word. *Tender* entered Middle English via Old French from the Latin root *tener*, "soft, delicate." In English, *tender* encompasses both God's capacity to "yield easily to force or pressure" in response to human fragility as well as humanity's "easily broken, divided, and injured" nature that yields to God's love.[60]

It is curious though that Coverdale, who reportedly did not read Greek or Hebrew, could have introduced such a felicitous English pairing that conveys the lexical form of the Hebrew *raḥămîm* as well as the emotional intensity and vulnerability associated with the Hebrew concept of compassionate mercy. In the prologue of his historic 1535 Bible, Coverdale explains that he consulted the Latin Vulgate and Sante Pagnini's Latin translation of the Psalms from Hebrew and Greek as well as German translations by Martin Luther and Ulrich Zwingli, though I have found no evidence that he derived the adjective *tender* from these sources. Coverdale may have been influenced by William Tyndale's translation of the New Testament published in 1534, in which he translates "splanchna eleous/viscera misericordiae" in Luke 1:78 and "splanchna oiktirmou/viscera misericordiae" in Colossians 3:12 as "tender mercy." There is no question of an underlying Hebrew term for these passages, since the New Testament was originally written in Greek, but the Greek terms that Tyndale translates come from the same constellation of terms that the Septuagint translators used for rendering *raḥămîm* in the Psalms—namely, *oiktirmós* and *eleos*—a fact Tyndale likely knew since he read Hebrew and Greek. Tyndale may have recognized genre conventions of psalms in Zacharias's song (Luke 1:68–79). Furthermore, Zacharias speaks of similar themes of deliverance and praise in this passage, closely aligning it with the Hebrew doctrine of *raḥămîm* and *ḥesed* in the Psalms. This passage from Luke would also have been well known throughout the Latin Middle Ages, since it was recited as the Canticle of Zacharias in the liturgy. As the Greek and Latin terms demonstrate, the physical, visceral notion embodied in *rḥm* were not effaced in this passage, primarily since the term for vitals

---

60. *Oxford English Dictionary*, s.v. "tender."

or organs was included. So perhaps Tyndale was the first to render the concept of *rḥm* in English as "tender mercy."

Could Tyndale have been the impetus for Coverdale's choice to translate *raḥămîm* in Psalm 25:6 as "tender mercies"? Although it is unknown where Coverdale made his biblical translation and where the first edition of the 1535 Bible was printed, David Daniell reports that Coverdale spent time in Antwerp in the early 1530s, where Tyndale was working and printing. There have been suggestions that Coverdale and Tyndale were associates, and Daniell believes they might have been, if for no other reason than they were both in Antwerp at the same time working on English Bible translations.[61] The circle of these scholars was not large. Although Coverdale did not know Hebrew, it is certainly possible that he was working with colleagues who may have pointed out to him the richer sense of *raḥămîm* that he had earlier missed in his metrical paraphrase.

The phrase *tender mercies* was used in subsequent sixteenth- and seventeenth-century bibles. Coverdale revised his 1535 translation of the Psalms for the royally approved Great Bible published in 1539; this version was adopted by Archbishop Thomas Cranmer as the psalter of the *Book of Common Prayer*, which was used by the Church of England until the twentieth century.[62] The popular Geneva Bible was translated by Marian exiles in 1560.[63] The Bishops' Bible was revised under the direction of Archbishop Matthew Parker in 1568 for use in the Church of England.[64] The King James Bible was completed in 1611 by a team of translators commissioned by King James.[65]

61. Daniell, *Bible in English*, 177–81.

62. Daniell, *Bible in English*, 198–220.

63. Daniell, *Bible in English*, 291–319.

64. Daniell, *Bible in English*, 338–47.

65. Daniell, *Bible in English*, 427–60. See also Campbell, *Bible*, and David Norton, *The King James Bible: A Short History from Tyndale to Today* (Cambridge: Cambridge University Press, 2011).

Geneva Bible: Remember, o Lorde, thy <u>tendre mercies</u>, and thy <u>louing kindenes</u>: for thei haue bene for euer.[66]

Bishops' Bible: Call to remembraunce O God thy <u>tender mercies</u> & thy <u>louyng kindnesse</u>: for they haue ben for euer.[67]

King James Bible: Remember, O Lord, thy <u>tender mercies</u>, and thy <u>louing kindnesses</u>: for they haue beene euer of old.[68]

By the end of the seventeenth century, the King James Bible (KJV) became the predominantly used Bible in England largely because the king's printer and then two privileged university presses held a monopoly on the publishing rights.[69] The consistency of the use of the phrase *tender mercies* in the major sixteenth-century biblical translations had so shaped English religious language that by the mid-sixteenth century, the phrase *tender mercies* appeared in sermons and other devotional writing.[70]

More than seventy different, new English versions of the Psalms were produced in the sixteenth century (see a representative sample of the metrical versions of Psalm 25:6 in the appendix at the end of this chapter). A significant number were composed by poets and clergy as they participated "in a long and relatively stable tradition of Christian devotion" that incorporated psalms in liturgical worship and private prayer.[71] The metrical versions particularly highlight the "intrinsic

---

66. *The Bible and Holy Scriptures conteyned in the Olde and Newe Testament. Translated according to the Ebrue and Greke, and conferred with the best translations in diuers langues* (Geneva, 1560), STC 2nd ed./2093, *EEBO*.

67. *The. holie. Bible conteynyng the olde Testament and the newe* (London, 1568), STC 2nd ed./2099, *EEBO*.

68. *The Holy Bible conteyning the Old Testament, and the New: newly translated out of the originall tongues: & with the former translations diligently compared and reuised, by his Maiesties speciall co[m]mandement* (London, 1611), STC 2nd ed./2216, *EEBO*.

69. Campbell, *Bible*, 108–28, 148.

70. For example, see sermons and writings by Thomas Becon, John Bradford, John Knox, and Thomas Lever. Searching "tender mercies" in *EEBO* produced 1,973 hits in 1,089 records.

71. Zim, *English Metrical Psalms*, 26.

affective appeal" of the "authoritative and eloquent texts" in the devotional practices of English Catholics and Protestants. The variety of translations for *raḥămîm* employed in the metrical psalms, such as "mercies manyfolde," and "louyng mercies," indicates that the pairing of "tender mercies" was not the inevitable translation. Over the century, the phrase *tender mercies* became sufficiently established for Sir Philip Sidney to engage in poetic word play in the 1580s, altering the familiar phrase to a possessive relationship: "Remember, only king, / Thy mercy's tenderness" in his lyric rendition of Psalm 25.[72] By the early seventeenth century, the translators of the KJV Psalms employed the conventional phrase *tender mercies* when rendering *raḥămîm*.

English-speaking colonists brought the King James Bible with them to America, and American printers began publishing editions of the KJV in 1777.[73] The KJV retained a central place in American religious life until 1901 when the official American Revised Version was published.[74] It has been well documented that antebellum American society and the Second Great Awakening movement were saturated with the language and images of the KJV and that Joseph Smith was likewise deeply immersed in the biblical culture of his family that centered on the KJV.[75] Consciously, unconsciously, or by inspiration, Joseph employs conventional scriptural idiom (that is, the language of the KJV) in his translation of the Book of Mormon.[76] As we have seen in this overview of the translations of Psalm 25:6, Joseph Smith's English scriptural idiom is encoded with linguistic and cultural

---

72. Sir Philip Sidney, "Psalm 25," lines 19–24, in *The Sidney Psalter: The Psalms of Sir Philip and Mary Sidney*, ed. Hannibal Hamlin et al. (Oxford: Oxford University Press, 2009), 47.

73. Daniell, *Bible in English*, 580–603.

74. Daniell, *Bible in English*, 624–58.

75. Philip L. Barlow, *Mormons and the Bible: The Place of Latter-day Saints in American Religion* (Oxford: Oxford University Press, 1991), 6, 14. See also John S. Tanner, "The King James Bible in America: Pilgrim, Prophet, President, Preacher," *BYU Studies* 50/3 (2011): 4–21; Kent P. Jackson, ed., *The King James Bible and the Restoration* (Salt Lake City: Deseret Book, 2011). See Marie Bourgerie Hunter, "Fossilized LDS Church Phrases in the Usage of Eliza R. Snow," *Schwa* 12 (April 2015): 20–22, for a corpora study of *tender mercies* in the nineteenth, twentieth, and twenty-first centuries.

76. See Barlow, *Mormons and the Bible*, 26–32.

hybridity. Tracing centuries of translations deepens our appreciation of how language mediates the transmission of theological concepts as they are reformed in new linguistic and cultural contexts and offers insight about Nephi's absent or inaccessible language.

The learning of Nephi's father: Empowering mercy in the Book of Mormon

Nephi frames his narration of his father's visions with self-reflective commentary about his purpose in making this particular record. Nephi will disclose in subsequent chapters (1 Nephi 6:1–6, 9:2–6, 10:1, 19) that this is not the first record that he has made of his people and that he received a divine mandate to make this record for a special and a wise purpose (9:2, 5). Before we learn these details though, Nephi introduces his theological project in verses 1 and 20, creating an inclusio, a thematic envelope, around the story of his father. In these verses, Nephi speaks directly to his audience, explaining that he makes his record to reveal his knowledge of God, more specifically of God's goodness and his mysteries—his tender mercies.

Nephi's theological project: The inclusio of 1:1 and 1:20b

Nephi begins his record by introducing two types of learning experiences in his life that have profoundly shaped his theological project. The syntactical structure of the first sentence illustrates the parallelism between parental and divine learning. Nephi describes his experiences in four participial clauses linked by the anaphora of "having." These descriptive statements are divided into two sections by causal clauses beginning "therefore."

> I Nephi,
> 1. having been born of goodly parents,
>   therefore I was taught somewhat in all the learning of my father; and,
> 2. having seen many afflictions in the course of my days, nevertheless

> 3. having been highly favored of the Lord in all my
>   days, yea
> 4. having had a great knowledge of the goodness and
>   the mysteries of God,
>   therefore I make a record of my proceedings in
>   my days. (1 Nephi 1:1)[77]

In the first clause, Nephi describes his parents as "goodly," because they provided a way for him to learn the social practices of his community. In the next sentence, Nephi specifies the content of his learning: "I make a record in the language of my father, which consists of the learning of the Jews and the language of the Egyptians" (1 Nephi 1:2); this linguistic, cultural, and religious literacy is crucial for Nephi to write a sacred record and to read and interpret other sacred records.

In the next three clauses, Nephi explains the rigorous method of divine tutoring. The contrast between the second and third clauses raises a question: Why does Nephi acknowledge suffering affliction while receiving divine favor? The fourth clause reveals the outcome of this paradoxical pedagogy: Nephi gains knowledge about God's nature, specifically his goodness and mysteries. Although afflictions are often interpreted as evidence of divine punishment, Nephi implies that gaining knowledge of God requires suffering, for it is in affliction that we seek God and that God powerfully manifests himself to us.[78] The repetition of the temporal phrases, "in the course of my days," "in all my days," and "proceedings of my days," suggests that Nephi's learning process unfolded over a lifetime rather than in discrete events. The attribute "good" seems to be an appropriate description of both his parents and God because of the care they demonstrate toward Nephi in endowing him with the knowledge he needs to make a true record memorializing his lifetime of learning.

Nephi's first example of divine tutoring comes not from his personal experience but from that of his father. Lehi hears prophecies of

---

77. I use Royal Skousen's *The Book of Mormon: The Earliest Text* (New Haven: Yale University Press, 2009), throughout, though I modify some of the punctuation.

78. Adam Miller discusses this divine mystery in his essay prepared for this volume.

the destruction of Jerusalem, and he prays to God "with all his heart" on "behalf of his people" (1 Nephi 1:5). A pillar of fire from which "he saw and heard much" appears to him (v. 6). Next, the "heavens open," and he sees God enthroned and surrounded by angels (v. 8). A brilliantly shining being brings him a book in which he reads about the destruction of Jerusalem. After reading and seeing "many great and marvelous things," Lehi joins the concourses of angels in praising God (vv. 14–15). Then Lehi joins the "many prophets," declaring "among the people" the knowledge he had acquired from God in his visions to his community and family (vv. 4, 18). However, "the Jews" reject his prophesies and threaten to kill him. At this critical moment in the narrative, Nephi pauses, leaving his audience in suspense as to whether Lehi would be "cast out and stoned and slain" as the "prophets of old," to remind us of his theological project (v. 20).

> But behold, I Nephi will shew you
>> that the tender mercies of the Lord is over all them,
>>> whom he hath chosen
>>> because of their faith,
>> to make them mighty,
>> even unto the power of deliverance. (v. 20)

The incongruity and dissonance between Lehi's plight and Nephi's thesis propel us into interpretive work. As we ponder how God will make Lehi "mighty, even unto the power of deliverance," we join the dialectic process in the narrative of learning about God through the characters' suffering of affliction and their exercising faith in becoming favored or chosen of God, just as Nephi introduced at the beginning of his record (see v. 1).

In addition to being a narrative crux, verse 20b is also a textual crux. We are accustomed to reading in the scriptures about the Lord delivering his chosen people, but the syntax in the verse does not suggest that the faithful are passively delivered. God offers an open invitation to all. Everyone may choose to be faithful to him, and in return God promises the faithful deliverance. However, the mechanism of this deliverance hinges upon the bestowal of tender mercies that seem to endow the faithful with some kind of potential power or ability to enact their deliverance. Nephi's conception of divine mercy seems to involve divine-human mutuality and reciprocity akin to the Hebrew concept of *raḥămîm* and Israel's theology of mercy articulated in the Psalms.

Praise and lament: Lehi, Nephi, and the language of the Psalms

As discussed above, the Hebrew word *raḥămîm* and its cognates frequently appear in the Psalms, so I consider broader resonances of psalms at the beginning of Nephi's record and how they may illuminate Nephi's theology of mercy. Since Nephi's or Lehi's records are not available in their original languages, any attempts at discerning intertextual allusions must remain speculative and must be filtered through the lens of Joseph Smith's scriptural idiom indebted to the KJV. Nevertheless, it may be productive to compare Nephi's theological statements and Lehi's direct discourse (or as much of what Nephi provides) with the language and imagery of the KJV psalms.

I suspect that Lehi's perception of his visions, or at least how he recorded them and taught them to his family, was infused with imagery from the psalms, the songs that generated ancient Israel's discourse for communicating with God. Although the received form of the Hebrew Psalter was not canonized until after Lehi's lifetime, it is likely that Lehi used similar songs as vehicles for praise and prayer in his cultic and devotional worship. John Goldingay surmises that "while the Psalms eventually do take a place in the context of individual spirituality and individual study, in origin many of them belong at least as intrinsically in the context of liturgical worship and priestly ministry, in the temple, in other sanctuaries, and later in the synagogue and other community settings for worship and ministry."[79] Other scholars suggest more specific associations of psalms with the temple in Jerusalem, where they probably functioned as libretto during temple worship.[80] For these reasons, it

---

79. Goldingay, *Psalms*, 46.

80. *The New Oxford Annotated Bible*, ed. Michael D. Coogan, 3rd ed. (Oxford: Oxford University Press, 2001), 775–76.

would not be surprising for Lehi to use language, images, and themes from the discourse of his worship to articulate his glimpses into heaven.

After relating Lehi's vision of God in majesty and the descent of a brilliant personage with a prophetic book, Nephi reports a brief exclamation of Lehi's praise. Nephi signals that Lehi has shifted into a special idiom with specific formal features when he explains, "after this manner was the language of my father in the praising of his God" (v. 15).[81] Lehi's praise follows the typical form of praise in biblical poetry: first a summons to praise, followed by reasons or motivations for praise.

> Great and marvelous are thy works, O Lord God
>   Almighty!
> Thy throne is high in the heavens,
> and thy power and goodness and mercy is over all the
>   inhabitants of the earth.
> And because thou art merciful,
> thou wilt not suffer those who come unto thee that
>   they shall perish. (1 Nephi 1:14)

In the summons of his first exclamation, Lehi responds with delight to God's nature and calls out to God with a string of sacred names. Then Lehi offers two reasons for his praise: God's sovereignty and his compassion. These statements employ structural parallelism, a formal feature of psalms.[82] First, God's lordship is illustrated by a visual image of his enthronement. Lehi amplifies this royal image in the second cola of the sentence by listing God's sovereign qualities. In the second reason, Lehi restates who God is with respect to his mercy and then defines what God does as a result of his mercy—he protects the faithful. There are certainly similarities between Lehi's praise at the conclusion of his vision of the heavenly council and Nephi's theology of mercy

---

81. Nephi uses this same descriptive phrase, "after this manner of language," when Sariah articulates her complaint and praise concerning her sons' dangerous trip to Jerusalem (1 Nephi 5:3, 8). I thank Julie M. Smith for this insight; see her "'I Will Sing to the Lord': Women's Songs in the Scriptures," *Dialogue* 45/3 (2012): 56–69.

82. See Goldingay, *Psalms*, 37–40.

in 1:20b. In particular, both Lehi and Nephi describe God's mercy as being "over all"; mercy is an essential element of God's nature.

> Thy power and goodness and **mercy is over all** the inhabitants of the earth. (1 Nephi 1:14)
>
> The tender **mercies** of the Lord **is over all** them. (1 Nephi 1:20)

Lehi's and Nephi's descriptions of God's merciful nature echo the laudatory KJV rendition of Psalm 145:8–9: "The Lord is gracious, and full of compassion; slow to anger, and of great mercy. The Lord is good to all: and his tender mercies are over all his works." They also anticipate Ammon's testimony of thanksgiving: "We see that God is mindful of every people.... His bowels of mercy are over all the earth" (Alma 26:37). Nephi's pluralization of *mercy* also may indicate that God's mercy is not a discrete response but an ongoing divine characteristic; God is always ready to respond to human suffering by experiencing *raḥămîm*, and "God performs *ḥesed* because he likes to do it.... It is his glory. He loves what he does and does what he loves. In recognizing this, we can begin to discern our true nature, desire to serve and deliver others."[83]

Although God's mercy is patiently steadfast and eternally available to all, Lehi and Nephi explain that not everyone will accept God's invitation to be in relation with him; humans choose to qualify and circumscribe God's mercy.

> Because thou art merciful, thou wilt not suffer those who come unto thee that they shall perish. (1 Nephi 1:14)
>
> Whom he hath chosen because of their faith to make them mighty, even unto the power of deliverance. (1 Nephi 1:20)

Human reciprocity demonstrated through obedience activates divine mercy. In both formulations, God exercises mercy by protecting the obedient, and in gratitude for deliverance (or anticipated deliverance), the obedient praise God. Nephi explains that Lehi was moved to praise

---

83. Belnap, "'How Excellent Is Thy Lovingkindness,'" 183.

at the end of his vision, "for his soul did rejoice and his whole heart was filled" (1 Nephi 1:15). In doing so Lehi imitated the "numberless concourses of angels" he had seen "in the attitude of singing and praising their God" at the beginning of his vision and may even have joined in their celestial song (v. 8). Together the angels and Lehi demonstrate that "praise is the duty and delight ... of all creation."[84]

But what should we make of Lehi's praise in light of the destruction he reads about in the heavenly book brought to him by the "one" (1 Nephi 1:9)? Nephi explains that his father "read concerning Jerusalem, that it should be destroyed and the inhabitants thereof; many should perish by the sword and many should be carried away captive into Babylon" (v. 13). The emotional impact of this devastation is heightened as Lehi quotes the book's lament: "Woe woe unto Jerusalem, for I have seen thine abominations" (v. 13; see also Jeremiah 13:27). Psalms offer examples and precedent for the stark juxtaposition of lament and praise in communication with God. As Walter Brueggemann explains, "Praise articulates and embodies our capacity to yield, submit, and abandon ourselves in trust and gratitude to the 'One' whose we are,"[85] for only when there is "articulation of hurt and anger, ... submission of them to God, and finally ... relinquishment ... can there be praise and acts of generosity."[86] John Goldingay likewise envisions the emotional attitudes of psalms as a circular spectrum cycling from praise to protest to plea to trust to thanksgiving to obedience and back to praise.[87] One function of psalms is to facilitate divine mercy on behalf of the psalmist. The psalmist calls God to feel *raḥămîm* and extend *ḥesed*; thus "the praise has the power to transform pain. But conversely, the present pain also keeps the act of praise honest."[88]

Lehi models this cyclical, maturing process of lament and praise in his vision. He initially seeks the Lord, to plead with his whole heart

---

84. Walter Brueggemann, *Israel's Praise: Doxology against Idolatry and Ideology* (Philadelphia: Fortress, 1988), 1.

85. Brueggemann, *Israel's Praise*, 1.

86. Brueggemann, *Israel's Praise*, 100.

87. Goldingay, *Psalms*, 68.

88. Brueggemann, *Israel's Praise*, 139.

on behalf of his people. God responds to Lehi's lament by revealing himself enthroned in heaven to Lehi and by sending "the one," whom Lehi will learn is a messiah and whom Nephi will learn is the Lamb of God. Yet this divine communion is complicated by the heavenly book in which Lehi reads about the imminent destruction of Jerusalem, at which point he echoes the book's lament for his community. Only after articulating this lament can he hear and vocalize the angelic praise. Lehi's laments generate contact with God, who responds by giving him knowledge that reorients his perspective about his personal and communal suffering, for which he offers God thanksgiving and praise. The responsive mutuality in Lehi's personal interaction with God is Nephi's initial evidence of God's tender mercies.

Lehi's life, especially in Nephi's account from 1 Nephi 1:4–20, reveals that articulating praise and lament are theological acts and social gestures that construct a theological world in which humans interact with God individually and communally. Lehi illustrates that as he approached God with candor about his suffering and with gratitude for his hope that God would respond mercifully, his relation with God deepened into a steadfast trust that mediated his mortal sorrows. This is precisely the relation conceptualized in the Hebrew terms *raḥămîm* and *ḥesed*, conveyed in English scriptural idiom as "tender mercies" and "loving kindnesses." God is moved with compassion for Lehi's suffering, so he offers Lehi empowering knowledge, knowledge that will frame his family's worship for generations and will protect his family from captivity in Babylon. Yet this knowledge also effects great suffering for Lehi and his family.

Nephi resumes his father's story after stating the theological thesis of his record in 1 Nephi 1:20. Lehi receives another vision in which the Lord commands him to "depart into the wilderness" (1 Nephi 2:1). Leaving Jerusalem preserves his life, but the consequence of his obedience and of God's deliverance is that Lehi and his family lose their home, inheritance, and wealth. Lehi spends the rest of his life barely surviving the rigors of traveling through deserts, sailing across the world, and founding a new civilization amid escalating violence among his sons. Though these sorrows weigh him even to death (1 Nephi 18:17–18; 2 Nephi 1:17), he receives (1) the comfort that "if I had not seen the things of God in a vision, I should not have known of the goodness of God but had tarried at Jerusalem and had perished with my brethren" (1 Nephi 5:4); (2) the promise that "notwithstanding our afflictions, we have obtained a land of promise, a land which is choice above all other lands, a land which the Lord God hath covenanted with me should be a land for the inheritance of my seed" (2 Nephi 1:5); and (3) the knowledge of his salvation: "the Lord hath redeemed my soul from hell. I have beheld his glory, and I am encircled about eternally in the arms of his love" (2 Nephi 1:15).[89] I suggest that these are the tender mercies that the Lord granted Lehi. This knowledge gave him the courage and fortitude to survive the dangers and the sorrows of his remarkable and unexpected life, so that he was made "mighty even unto the power of deliverance" (1 Nephi 1:20). According to Nephi, God does not deliver the faithful by miraculous intervention; instead, God empowers the obedient with the knowledge, means, and strength necessary to survive, to grow, and even to flourish.[90]

Nephi continues to develop his theology of mercy as he tells of his own tender mercies and as he interprets prophesies in Isaiah with respect to his family's future. For example, Nephi obtains precious scripture and family history on the brass plates but has to kill Laban for them (1 Nephi 3–4); he and his family survive an eight-year desert journey but are sustained by raw meat (1 Nephi 17:1–4); and they are pledged a promised land but have to build a seaworthy boat and traverse oceans to get there (1 Nephi 17–18). Divine mercies empower deliverance, but they also often involve (in Nephi's record) suffering affliction. Nephi's tender mercies are not sweet coincidences or reassuring serendipity, but

---

89. Nephi employs the phrase *tender mercies* when he describes Lehi's vision of the tree of life. In 1 Nephi 8:8, Nephi repeats (or quotes) Lehi's desperation after wandering for what seemed like hours in darkness and then praying to the Lord to have mercy upon him, "according to the multitude of his tender mercies." Lehi's prayer is answered by seeing a tree "whose fruit was desirable to make one happy." Nephi will eventually learn that this tree represents "the love of God, which sheddeth itself abroad in the hearts of the children of men; wherefore it is the most desirable above all things.... Yea, and the most joyous to the soul" (11:22–23). God's condescension is manifest most particularly in Jesus Christ, the Lamb of God, the Son of the Eternal Father, who was born a human to be slain for the sins of the world (11:32).

90. Compare the repetition of God providing the "means" to achieve commandments in 1 Nephi 3:7 and 17:3. I thank Ben Huff for this insight.

very type of afflictions that spur painful maturation, the rigorous stage of the transformation of weakness into strength.

Conclusion: Nephi's invitation

In the first chapter of Nephi's record, he introduces his theological project to produce a record that reveals and testifies of a particular form of divine-human relations characterized by "tender mercies," in which suffering affliction and knowing God are interlinked. In narrating his father's story, Nephi illustrates how humans invite divine beings to participate in their mortal experiences and how divine beings invite humans to participate in the sacred story of salvation. In doing so, Nephi invites us to live within and through scriptural narrative by recognizing tender mercies in scriptural stories and then examining our own lives for evidence of divine mercy. Like Nephi and Joseph Smith, we should make a record in our own language, according to our learning, to record God's tender mercies in the afflictions of our own lives, the lives of our families, our neighborhoods, wards, nations, and world. As we come to recognize how God participates in our life, we take part in God's life in the unfolding narrative of salvation.[91]

---

91. I thank Don Chapman for his enriching suggestions during the composition of this paper.

Appendix: Translations of Psalm 25:6

Sources	Dates	Texts
Hebrew Bible	400–500s BC	זְכֹר־רַחֲמֶיךָ יְהוָה וַחֲסָדֶיךָ כִּי מֵעוֹלָם הֵמָּה׃
Septuagint	200–300s BC	(24:6) μνήσθητι τῶν οἰκτιρμῶν σου κύριε καὶ τὰ ἐλέη σου ὅτι ἀπὸ τοῦ αἰῶνός εἰσιν
Vulgate, Jerome	AD 380–90s	[Romanum] Reminiscere miserationum tuarum domine et misericordia tua quae a saeculo sunt.
		[Gallican] Reminiscere miserationum tuarum domine et misericordiarum tuarum quae a seculo sunt.
		[Hebraicum] Reminiscere miserationum tuarum domine atque misericordiarum tuarum: quod a seclo sunt.
Vespasian Psalter	mid-800s	(24:5) Gemyne mildsa ðinra dryht[en] & mildheortnis ðin ða from werulde sind.
Paris Psalter	c. 1050	(24:5) Gemun, Drihten, þinra miltsunga and þinre mildheortnesse þe fram fruman worlde wæs.
Surtees Psalter	c. 1250–1300	(24:6) Lauerd, ofe þine reuthes mine þou mare, And of þine milþes, of world þat are.
Psalter, Richard Rolle	c. 1340	(24:6) Vmthynke ye of thi mercyingis lord; and of thi mercys, the whilke ere fra the warld.
West Midlands Prose Psalter	c. 1350	(24:6) By-þenche þe, Lord, of þy pites and of þy mercies þat ben of þe world.
Wycliffite Bible Psalters	c. 1370s–1380s	[Earlier Version] Recorde of thi mercy deedis, Lord; and of thi mercies that fro the world ben.
		[Later Version] Lord, haue thou mynde of thi merciful doyngis; and of thi mercies that ben fro the world.

---

1. In 1534, George Joye produced another psalm paraphrase, *David's Psalter,* translating Ulrich Zwingli's Latin (1532): "Remember thy mercy and goodnes: which thou of euer vseste." See Zim, *English Metrical Psalms,* 214.

2. Martin Bucer, *Psalmorum libri quinque ad ebraicam veritatem versi* (1529), 139.

Sources	Dates	Texts
The Psalter of David in Englyshe, George Joye	1530	Lorde remembre thy mercy and thy gracious favoure: for in theis thynges thou excellest euen from the begynnynge.[1]
		Martin Bucer: Memor sis misericordiae tuae Autophyes, & benignitatis tuae, quando quidem iis praestas ab initio.[2]
A Paraphrasis, Miles Coverdale	1534, 1535	Call to remembraunce Lorde thy kyndnesse & gentylnesse, whyche in fore tymes thou hast used so liberally towarde those that are thyne.
		Jan van Campen: Reuoca in memoriam Domine clementiam & benignitatem tuam, quibus seculis superioribus tam liberaliter usus es erga tuos.
Coverdale Bible, Miles Coverdale	1535	Call to remembraunce, O LORDE, thy tender mercyes & thy louinge kyndnesses, which haue bene euer of olde.
The manuall of prayers, Church of England	1539	Call vnto remembraunce (O Lorde) thy tender mercyes, and thy louynge kindnesses which haue ben euer of olde.[3]
An Epitome of the Psalms, Richard Taverner	1539	but rather thynke on thy tender mercye which thou hast continued towards those that thou haste chosen from the begynnynge of the worlde, neyther is there any man that can stoppe the from thyne accustomed wonte.[4]

3. Church of England, *The manuall of prayers, or the prymer in Englyshe set out at lengthe, whose contentes the reader by the prologe next after the kalendar, shal sone perceaue and there in shal se brefly the order of the whole boke. Set forth by Ihon late bysshope of Rochester at the co[m]aundement the ryght honorable Lorde Thomas Cro[m]wel, Lorde Priuie seale Uicegerent to the Kynges hyghnes* (London, 1539), STC 2nd ed./16010, *EEBO*.

4. Richard Taverner, trans., *An epitome of the Psalmes, or briefe meditacions vpon the same, with diuerse other moste christian prayers, translated by Richard Tauerner* (London, 1539), STC 2nd ed./2748, *EEBO*.

5. *The Byble in Englyshe that is to saye, the content of all the holye scrypture, bothe of the olde and newe Testament, truly translated after the veryte of the Hebrue and Greke textes, by the diligent studye of dyuers excellent lerned [men e]xperte in the fore[saide] tongues* (London, 1640), STC 2nd ed./2069, *EEBO*.

6. Robert Crowley, trans., *The Psalter of Dauid newely translated into Englysh metre in such sort that it maye the more decently, and wyth more delyte of the mynde, be reade and songe of al men* (1549), *EEBO*. See also Zim, *English Metrical Psalms*, 134.

7. Church of England, *The booke of common prayer, and adminystracion of the sacramentes, and other rites and ceremonies in the Churche of Englande* (London, 1553), STC 2nd ed./16288a, *EEBO*.

Sources	Dates	Texts
Great Bible	1540	Call to remembraunce (O Lorde) thy tender mercyes, and thy louynge kindnesses, which haue bene euer of olde.[5]
Psalter of David, Robert Crowley	1549	Remember thy mercyes (O lorde) & eke thy greate goodnes: for sence the worlde was fyrste create, they dyd yet neuer cease.[6]
Book of Common Prayer	1553	Cal to remembraunce (O Lord) thy tender mercyes: and thy louing kindnes, which hath been euer of olde.[7]
Certayne Psalmes, Thomas Sternhold	1549 [1562]	Thy mercies manyfolde, I praye the lorde remembre, And eke thy pitie plentifull, That doeth indure foreuer.[8]
Geneva Bible	1560	Remember, o Lorde, thy tendre mercies, and thy louing kindenes: for thei haue bene for euer.
Metrical Psalter, Matthew Parker	1567	Call thou to mynde: O Lord full kynde, Thy louyng mercies olde: Thy bounties free: which euer bee, As fathers them have tolde.[9]
Bishops' Bible	1568	Call to remembraunce O God thy tender mercies & thy louyng kindnesse: for they haue ben for euer.

---

8. Thomas Sternhold, trans., *The whole booke of Psalmes collected into Englysh metre by T. Starnhold, I. Hopkins, & others, conferred with the Ebrue, with apt notes to synge the[m] with al; faithfully perused and alowed according to thordre appointed in the Quenes Maiesties iniunctions ; very mete to be vsed of all sortes of people priuately for their solace & comfort, laying apart all vngodly songes and ballades, which tende only to the norishing of vyce, and corrupting of youth* (London, 1562), STC 2nd ed./2430, *EEBO*. In *English Metrical Psalms*, 112–27, Zim explains that Thomas Sternhold, groom of the King's Robes, translated a selection (19–37) of psalms and offered them as "holye songes of veritie" to the pious Edward VI and his court. The publication of Sternhold's *Certayne Psalmes* in 1549 sparked a flurry of metrical psalm productions. Sternhold's translations were adopted by John Calvin's congregation in Geneva: *The forme of prayers and ministration of the sacraments, &c. vsed in the Englishe Congregation at Geneua and approued, by the famous and godly learned man, Iohn Caluyn* (Geneua, 1556), STC 2nd ed./16561, *EEBO*.

9. Matthew Parker, trans., *The whole Psalter translated into English metre* (London, 1567), 57, STC 2nd ed./2729, *EEBO*. While in retirement during the reign of Queen Mary, Matthew Parker, who would become Elizabeth's first Archbishop of Canterbury, composed a metrical psalter in 1556 employing a variety of stanzaic verse forms to be sung to the eight tunes composed by Thomas Tallis accompanying his *Psalter*; see Zim, *English Metrical Psalms*, 135–39.

Sources	Dates	Texts
Sidney Psalter, Philip Sidney	1580s	Remember, only king, Thy mercy's tenderness: To thy remembrance bring Thy kindness, lovingness. Let those things thy remembrance grave, Since they eternal essence have.
The key of the holy tongue, John Udall	1593	Remember thy manifold compassions o lord, and mercies that they haue beene of old.[10]
King James Bible	1611	Remember, O Lord, thy tender mercies, and thy louing kindnesses: for they haue beene euer of old.
Bay Psalm Book	1640	Thy bowels, Lord, & thy mercyes minde; for they are for aye.[11]
King James Bible, ed. Benjamin Blayney	1769	Remember, O LORD, thy tender mercies and thy lovingkindnesses; for they have been ever of old.[12]

---

10. John Udall, *Mafteah leshon ha-kodesh that is The key of the holy tongue wherein is conteineid, first the Hebrue grammar (in a manner) woord for woord out of P. Martinius* (Leyden, 1593), STC 2nd ed./17523, *EEBO*. See also Zim, *English Metrical Psalms*, 255.

11. *The whole booke of psalmes faithfully translated into English metre* ([Cambridge, MA], 1640), STC 2nd ed./2738, *EEBO*.

12. *The Holy Bible, containing the Old and New Testaments* (Oxford, 1769), ESTCT91970, *EECO*.

Joining the Heavenly Chorus

Michaël Ulrich

THE BEGINNING OF THE BOOK OF MORMON is interesting in many regards. It contains the record of two visions received by Lehi: the first consisting of a "pillar of fire" on "a rock before him" (1 Nephi 1:6), and the second consisting of the vision of God himself and his entourage (vv. 8–15). First-time readers are almost always impressed by the grandeur of Lehi's vision of the throne of God. However, a closer examination of this first chapter leads us to question why Nephi included such a detail, especially given his repeated concern about "not mak[ing] a full account of the things which [his] father hath written" (v. 16). Why did Nephi choose to elaborate on the second vision, the throne theophany,[1] and not detail the things seen and heard in the first vision, the pillar of fire? While the definitive answer to such questions will always remain inaccessible—only Nephi could tell us his reasons—I will argue that one possible reason[2] is that the revelations Nephi received in 1 Nephi 11 can be seen, in part, as

---

1. For more on the throne theophany, see Blake T. Ostler, "The Throne-Theophany and Prophetic Commission in 1 Nephi: A Form-Critical Analysis," *BYU Studies* 26/4 (1986): 67–95.

2. Joseph M. Spencer suggests in his book *An Other Testament: On Typology* (Provo, UT: Maxwell Institute, 2016) that one goal Nephi may have had in mind when he began writing his record could have been to give an account of the beginnings of the Nephite people and, thus, legitimate their line of kings. In this regard, Nephi may have decided to mention in greater detail the throne theophany because it would obviously demonstrate that Lehi was a prophet and thus legitimize Lehi's and Nephi's authority.

divinely given interpretations of Lehi's throne theophany. Taking this approach, we may better understand in general how revelation should be received in order for us to come to God and, figuratively, join along with Lehi in the chorus of angels.

We must first understand the pattern set in Lehi's grand vision in order to be able to recognize it in Nephi's own visions. Lehi's vision of the throne of God, situated in verses 8 through 15 of 1 Nephi 1, consists of the following elements: Lehi is "carried away in a vision" and sees "the heavens open"; he sees the throne of God and hosts of angels praising God; one angel comes down, followed by twelve others, and gives him a book from which he is commanded to read; Lehi reads a prophecy of the destruction of Jerusalem and finally joins the angels by praising God.

Second, in order to see the relationship of this vision to that in 1 Nephi 11, we must understand the context of this latter chapter. In 1 Nephi 8, Lehi, a "visionary man," has received his dream of the tree of life after his flight from Jerusalem. His son Nephi then wants to see that vision for himself and to get an interpretation of it. As a result, Nephi is given a lengthy and comprehensive revelation beginning in chapter 11 that extends through chapter 14. My claim is that we can see in 1 Nephi 11–12 five different visions that fit into the pattern of Lehi's previous throne theophany. This claim rests on the use of similar structures and similar phrases, as table 1 shows.[3]

Table 1. Parallels between 1 Nephi 11–12 and the throne theophany of 1 Nephi 1

	1 Nephi 11–12	**1 Nephi 1**
First vision (1 Nephi 11:1–9)	"I sat pondering" (v. 1)	"he cast himself upon his bed, being overcome with the Spirit" (v. 7)
	"I was caught away" (v. 1)	"he was carried away" (v. 8)
	"into an exceedingly high mountain" (v. 1)	"he saw the heavens open" (v. 8)

---

3. Please note that the quotations in the tables follow the wording of Royal Skousen's *The Book of Mormon: The Earliest Text* (New Haven: Yale University Press, 2009).

	1 Nephi 11–12	1 Nephi 1
	the Spirit praises the Lord (v. 6)	Lehi praises the Lord (v. 14)
	"God over all the earth" (v. 6)	"thy power and goodness and mercy is over all the inhabitants of the earth" (v. 14)
	"even above all" (v. 6)	"Thy throne is high in the heavens" (v. 14)
	"blessed art thou Nephi because thou believest" (v. 6)	"thou wilt not suffer those who come unto thee that they shall perish!" (v. 14)
	"a man descending out of heaven" (v. 7)	"one descending out of the midst of heaven" (v. 9)
	"beauty" and "whiteness" (v. 8); "precious" (v. 9)	"luster" and "brightness" (vv. 9–10)
Second vision (1 Nephi 11:13–24)	"exceeding fair and white" (v. 13)	"luster" and "brightness" (vv. 9–10)
	"I saw the heavens open" (v. 14)	"he saw the heavens open" (v. 8)
	"an angel came down and stood before me" (v. 14)	"and the first came and stood before my father" (v. 11)
	"she was carried away in the Spirit" (v. 19)	"he was carried away" (v. 8)
	"the Son of God a going forth among the children of men" (v. 24)	"they . . . went forth upon the face of the earth" (v. 11)
Third vision (1 Nephi 11:27–29)	"I beheld the heavens open" (v. 27)	"he saw the heavens open" (v. 8)
	"the Holy Ghost came down out of heaven" (v. 27)	"one descending out of the midst of heaven" (v. 9)
	"he went forth" (v. 28)	"they . . . went forth upon the face of the earth" (v. 11)

(table continues)

Table 1 (*continued*)

	1 Nephi 11–12	1 Nephi 1
	"I also beheld twelve others following him" (v. 29)	"and he also saw twelve others following him" (v. 10)
	"they were carried away in the Spirit" (v. 29)	"he was carried away" (v. 8)
Fourth vision (1 Nephi 11:30–36)	"I beheld the heavens open" (v. 30)	"he saw the heavens open" (v. 8)
	"I saw angels descending" (v. 30)	"one descending out of the midst of heaven" (v. 9)
	"the Lamb of God going forth among the children of men" (v. 31)	"they ... went forth upon the face of the earth" (v. 11)
Fifth vision (1 Nephi 12:6–10)	"I saw the heavens open" (v. 6)	"he saw the heavens open" (v. 8)
	"the Lamb of God descending out of heaven" (v. 6)	"one descending out of the midst of heaven" (v. 9)
	"twelve others" (v. 7)	"and he also saw twelve others following him" (v. 10)

What are we to make of these similarities? While certain phrases and expressions could certainly be used to describe many different visions (e.g., "I saw the heavens open" or "he was carried away") and are therefore not conclusive, we can here observe a deep similarity of specific patterns (the presence of a mediator coming down from heaven, whether it be an angel, the Spirit, or Christ himself; the notion of "going forth"; the idea of beauty, luster; etc.). Of course, some of these visions have stronger parallels with the book's first chapter than others, and some elements of Lehi's throne theophany are not present in all these visions: for instance, the shout of praise appears only in Nephi's first vision.

It thus seems that Nephi's vision—at least the part contained in chapter 11 and the beginning of chapter 12—can be seen as divinely given interpretations not only of the dream of the tree of life but also of his father's throne theophany. The division into five visions may be read as five different interpretations of Lehi's grand vision. Table 2 sums up the teachings received by Nephi.

Note that the first vision of Nephi is unusual because it is the only one in which the person who sees the vision (in other words, the person who takes up the role played by Lehi in the throne theophany) is not Nephi himself but rather the Spirit, as can be seen both by the fact that the Spirit is the one to praise the Lord and by the fact that he is the one talking about "a man descending out of heaven" (1 Nephi 11:7). Nephi will testify about this man later—but only later.

We should also note, as previously mentioned, that not all the elements of Lehi's vision are present in each one of Nephi's. For instance, there is no trace of anyone being "carried away" in the fifth vision. Similarly, in the fourth vision this element may be present only in the description of the Son of God being "lifted up upon the cross" (1 Nephi 11:33). But still, it is not an explicit repetition of Lehi's being carried away.

The main point is that many elements of the throne theophany appear to be identified with very different figures. The "one descending" is, for instance, an angel, a group of angels, the Spirit, or Jesus Christ, as identified through one of his titles. This method of interpretation takes up Lehi's vision as a general pattern to understand and explain a certain vision of world history (the coming of the Messiah— who would be born of Mary, would be rejected, and would appear to his people in America, etc.),[4] and this pattern can be used to explain different parts of this history.

Readers of the Book of Mormon are faced with the same kinds of questions as Nephi when confronted with Lehi's visions and dreams: What are we to make of them? How are we to understand them? How are we to apply them in our lives? Nephi's own response to these questions models one approach: read Lehi's visions as a pattern giving meaning both to history at large and to our own individual lives.

But what of the heavenly choir? One of the most striking features of Lehi's throne theophany was the "numberless concourses of angels in the attitude of singing and praising their God" (1 Nephi 1:8). Is there

---

4. The whole of Nephi's vision, from chapter 11 to chapter 14, is about world history, particularly about the history of the yet-to-be Lehite nations.

Table 2. Teachings received by Nephi in his visions compared to Lehi's vision

	Lehi's vision	First vision	Second vision	Third vision	Fourth vision	Fifth vision
The one who sees the vision	Lehi	the Spirit	Nephi	Nephi	Nephi	Nephi
One carried away	Lehi	Nephi	the mother of the Son of God	the apostles	(the Lamb of God?)	–
One descending	"one descending out of the midst of heaven"	the Son of God	an angel	the Holy Ghost	angels	the Lamb of God
One going forth	"twelve others"	–	the Son of God	the Lamb of God	the Lamb of God	–
One who praises	Lehi	the Spirit	–	–	–	–
Twelve others	"twelve others following him"	–	–	the apostles	–	the twelve Nephite disciples

an equivalent to this aspect in Nephi's visions? The Spirit is praising the Lord in Nephi's first vision, but here only one person is praising. One person is far removed from "numberless concourses."

This element—the praising hosts of God's heavenly council—is a pivotal element in Lehi's vision. All of 1 Nephi 1 can be read as a conversion story, the story of Lehi's spiritual growth. At the beginning of the chapter, Lehi finds himself in a wicked and sinful setting.[5] Lehi then begins his spiritual journey by receiving a first revelation in the form of a pillar of fire that leaves him "overcome with the Spirit" (v. 7). This time may be seen as a spiritual preparation for the second vision that shortly follows, his vision of the throne of God. At the end of this vision, we see Lehi in verse 14 joining the chorus of angels in songs of praise. To summarize, we follow Lehi on a journey[6] from a sinful location to heaven and its hosts. His journey illustrates how the believer, undergoing the process of conversion and sanctification, can finally come to join the heavenly hosts, the chorus of angels, and like them "speak with the tongue of angels and shout praises unto the Holy One of Israel" (2 Nephi 31:13). As a result, it will be critical to see if Nephi has anything to tell us in his own revelatory interpretation of Lehi's vision about how to undergo this process.

My hypothesis is that we can indeed find this element—Lehi's numberless concourses of praising angels—in Nephi's vision, but in an inverted form: they show up in the figure of the "great and spacious building" of Lehi's dream. This building appears for the first time in verse 26 of chapter 8 in Lehi's account of his dream. There are many elements in favor of a comparison between the hosts of heaven and the hosts of scorning people. The building is described in chapter 8 as standing "in the air, high above the earth" (1 Nephi 8:26), which echoes the heavenly location of the angelic hosts (1 Nephi 1:8). The

---

5. The text tells us little about Lehi's previous spiritual state. We know that Nephi's parents were "goodly," and it thus seems improbable that Lehi was as much stuck in sin as his contemporaries. At any rate, the overall spiritual state of Jerusalem is one of wickedness and sin, as indicated by the message delivered by the prophets in 1 Nephi 1:4.

6. The initiatory character of Lehi's experience—and of Nephi's—is reinforced by the presence of mediators, whether it be "one descending out of the midst of heaven," the Spirit, or an angel, whose function it is to accompany them in their spiritual journey.

people are also described as being dressed in an "exceeding fine" manner (1 Nephi 8:27), which could perhaps be compared to the "luster" and "brightness" characterizing divine beings (1 Nephi 1:9–10). And whereas the inhabitants of the building are "in the attitude of mocking and pointing their fingers" (1 Nephi 8:27), the angels are "in the attitude of singing and praising their God" (1 Nephi 1:8).

The result of the mocking is that many people who have come to the tree of life and beheld the scene are feeling "ashamed" (1 Nephi 8:28), whereas Lehi, the spectator of God's council, is "filled with the Spirit" (1 Nephi 1:12) and "his whole heart [is] filled" (v. 15). And, whereas heavenly beings descend (v. 9) or "[go] forth" (v. 11), which denotes an ordered, intended, controlled movement, the spectators of the building "[fall] away into forbidden paths and [are] lost" (1 Nephi 8:28), which denotes a chaotic, unintentional movement.

We thus see two possible responses to revelation: one, exemplified by Lehi, that leads to joining the praising hosts, and another, exemplified by the "multitudes pressing their way towards that great and spacious building" (1 Nephi 8:31), that leads to joining the scorning hosts. The former are the masters of their fate, as described by the idea of ordered and intended motion, while the latter are driven against their will, as indicated by the notion of chaotic, unintentional movement. For believers to understand the difference between these two responses and, in particular, how to imitate Lehi's response is crucial.

Laying aside for a moment the "great and spacious building," we want to focus on the means used by Lehi in 1 Nephi 1 to receive his vividly sensorial revelations. Etymologically, the word *reveal* comes from Latin and means "to draw back the veil." Revelation involves perceiving what could not be perceived, seeing the invisible, hearing the unutterable, and reading the unreadable, and therefore it is grounded in the senses. What senses are used by Lehi to receive his revelations in 1 Nephi 1? We find a sensory triad of hearing, seeing, and reading. These are the means by which Lehi is able to get knowledge through revelation. More precisely, table 3 illustrates occurrences of these senses as related to Lehi:

Table 3. Sensory events in Lehi's revelations of 1 Nephi 1

To hear	"he saw and **heard** much" (v. 6); "which he saw and **heard**" (v. 6); "which he had both seen and **heard**" (v. 18); "which he saw and **heard**" (v. 19)	4 occurrences
To see	"he **saw** and heard much" (v. 6); "which he **saw** and heard" (v. 6); "the things which he had **seen**" (v. 7); "even that he **saw** the heavens open" (v. 8); "he **saw** God" (v. 8); "he **saw** one" (v. 9); "he **beheld**" (v. 9); "he also **saw** twelve others" (v. 10); "my father had read and **saw**" (v. 14); "the things which he had **seen**" (v. 15); "the Lord had **shewn** unto him" (v. 15); "he **saw** in visions and in dreams" (v. 16); "the Lord had **shewn** so many marvelous things unto my father, Lehi" (v. 18); "which he had both **seen** and heard" (v. 18); "which he **saw** and heard" (v. 19)	15 occurrences
To read	"that he should **read**" (v. 11); "as he **read**" (v. 12); "and he **read**" (v. 13); "did my father **read**" (v. 13); "my father had **read** and saw" (v. 14); "which he **read** in the book" (v. 19)	6 occurrences

Of the three senses, Lehi uses vision most often, whereas hearing is the least represented. The first vision, the vision of the pillar of fire, entails only hearing and seeing, and reading comes into play only in the second vision, the throne theophany.

Can we understand something from the different senses used? There is indeed a difference of involvement on the part of the perceiving subject between these three senses. Hearing is the most passive sense and does not even necessarily imply active listening. When there is a sound or a noise, there is no other choice than to hear it. Seeing, on the other hand, demands much more on the part of the subject. It requires turning the head in the right direction and keeping the eyes open. Reading is the most active of the whole triad and requires a high degree of physical and mental involvement: it is necessary to look at the text, to follow the lines with the eyes, and to mentally transform the script into words and those combinations of words into meaning. Thus the succession of Lehi's two visions charts an increase in his level of active involvement: he first hears and sees, and then he sees and even reads.

His active involvement demonstrates his commitment to receiving the knowledge the Lord wants to give him and deeply involves him in the revelatory process.

This increasing involvement is shown not only by the sensory triad but is also reflected in other parts of the text. In the vision of the pillar of fire, this pillar just rests on a rock "before him," whereas the second vision encompasses him so that he stands, in a sense, in the midst of it. And of course his greatest involvement comes when he joins the heavenly council by shouting praises and declaring the judgments of God: "Woe woe unto Jerusalem, for I have seen thine abominations" (1 Nephi 1:13).

In this regard, it is interesting to compare Lehi's high degree of involvement in receiving the Lord's will with the involvement of the people to whom he preaches at Jerusalem. The only sensory verb used in connection with the people is "hearing" in 1 Nephi 1:20: "And when the Jews heard these things, they were angry with him." The people do not proactively receive revelation. Rather, they passively hear what is said. Remaining passive, they are not able to see the invisible, hear the unutterable, and read the unreadable. In short, they are not able to receive what the Lord intends to give them. Instead, they pursue their course downward by not receiving the revelation and eventually become angry with the revelator and "[seek] his life" (1 Nephi 1:20).

How are we to compare these experiences—both that of Lehi and that of Jerusalem's people—with those of the crowd in the "great and spacious building"? The angel explains to Nephi in 1 Nephi 12:18 that this building represents the "vain imaginations and the pride of the children of men." Imagination is the ability to see things in one's own mind, to represent concepts and ideas in one's own mind. Imagination is not bad per se. As readers, we need imagination in the process of reading scriptures in order to be able to represent in our own minds the things we are reading, to attribute meaning to them, and finally to be able to see our own lives reflected in them. Imagination is one means used by the Spirit to help us read our own lives into the scriptures. In fact, the best proof of the importance of imagination may be given in 1 Nephi 5. Sariah, fearing for the life of her children, accused her husband Lehi of being a "visionary man" (1 Nephi 5:2). This sounds like

a harsh accusation, but Lehi does not counter it. He recognizes that
he is a "visionary man," and he even feels blessed to have this ability:
"I know that I am a visionary man, for if I had not seen the things of
God in a vision, I should not have known the goodness of God but had
tarried at Jerusalem and had perished with my brethren" (1 Nephi 5:4).

But the kind of imagination at stake in the great and spacious
building is qualified. How does *vain* qualify *imagination* in 1 Nephi
12:18? The adjective *vain* denotes something that is pointless or useless,
or it means to have an exceedingly high opinion of one's own abilities.
We could say that an imagination is vain if it is grounded in pride,
in our own representations of ourselves and of the world, so that we
refuse to let the Lord, through his revelations, give us a more correct
image of ourselves that would allow us to repent. A vain imagination
is therefore useless because it does not allow us to change, nor is it
led by the Spirit. We remain stuck in our own worldview, refusing to
see ourselves in the scriptures. In the language of Ether 12:6, where
Moroni describes faith as "things which are hoped for and not seen," we
could compare vain imagination to a "faithful imagination." Whereas
a faithful imagination is to see things that are invisible but nevertheless real and can therefore be accessed only by revelation, having vain
imagination is to see things that are invisible precisely because they
are unreal and are therefore seen only through the distorting mirror
of prideful imagination.

The revelations of God are by nature disturbing in that they force
us to view ourselves in a way that differs from our own conceptions
and sometimes even contradicts them harshly. These revelations give
us a mirror in which we can see "things as they really are" (Jacob 4:13).
Our imagination will be useful only if it helps us to look in this mirror,
thus allowing God to change our own opinions in order to introduce a
spiritual worldview. If not, our imagination will only be vain.

Notably, the "great and spacious building" has no foundation: it
is just standing in the air. It has no connections whatsoever with the
earth. Do we learn anything about the relationship between the earth
and the location of the praising angels in 1 Nephi 1? The text is not
explicit on this matter. Nevertheless, the "pillar of fire" seen by Lehi
in his first vision is reminiscent of the pillars that hold the heavens

above the earth in the imagery of the ancients. If we allow such an interpretation for a moment, what implications can we draw about the relationship between vain imagination and faithful imagination? A faithful imagination allows us to see things invisible but nevertheless real, things that connect with our daily experience. A faithful imagination is not interested in pure metaphysical speculations without reference to our practical duties as Christians. It also does not involve seeing the future without some connection to the present. God may, for instance, grant us a vision of our eternal potential, but this vision does not deny the reality of our current need to repent because of our mortality. On the other hand, vain imaginations have no connection with reality. They deny our need for repentance. They flatter us with either a false vision of being perfect or a feeling of being hopelessly lost. In any case, vain imaginations convince us that we are totally independent and don't need God to achieve a state of greater happiness. This vain idea of independence from God is strengthened by the fact that the multitudes in the great and spacious building are mocking the others outside. Indeed, if someone is mocking, he implicitly takes himself as the metric by which other people should be measured. They are not following the same road that he, in his "great and spacious building," is pursuing; therefore, they are less than he is! But it is different in the heavenly choirs that praise God. Praise takes someone else as the measure for what is good. The "numberless concourses of angels" praising God take him as the right metric by which humanity should be measured. This contrast leads to a second opposition: vain imagination as opposed to "praising imagination." In that sense, people with a vain imagination believe that they are independent of everybody and everything else because they are the measure. But people with a "praising imagination" recognize that they are dependent on God because he is their measure. This notion of vain independence may also be linked with another "great and spacious building": the tower of Babel. The tower of Babel was built because people thought they could be like God without needing to rely on God.

This opposition appears to be at work in the different responses to afflictions shown by Nephi on one hand and by Laman and Lemuel on the other. There is no question that Lehi's family experienced great hardships: leaving Jerusalem and all of their earthly possessions, living several years in the wilderness, and eating "raw meat" (1 Nephi 17:2). But to these hard circumstances, the brothers' reactions are diametrically opposed. Nephi sees in them the blessings of the Lord. He says right from the beginning that he has "been highly favored of the Lord in all [his] days" (1 Nephi 1:1). He even goes so far as to see eating raw meat as one of the "blessings of the Lord" because it was another way for God to show his power. Even though they ate raw meat, their "women did give plenty of suck for their children" (1 Nephi 17:2). On the other side, Laman and Lemuel always look at the afflictions themselves but not beyond. They complain about their circumstances, their sufferings, and "[their] women hav[ing] toiled, being big with child"; they even go on to say that "it would have been better" to suffer death itself (1 Nephi 17:20). Laman and Lemuel take themselves as the measure for their experience: we have suffered and that is all that counts. Nothing can change that. Nothing can redeem that. On the other hand, Nephi looks at the Lord as the measure: yes, I have suffered, but this suffering has been redeemed by the blessings received because even

my sufferings have helped me to better understand God. Thus, while believers act based on faith, taking God as the measure of things, unbelievers act based on pride and take themselves as the measure of things.

In conclusion, it seems that the only adequate response to revelations from the Lord is to actively engage with them. We must see them as a pattern through which we can look on life so we can give

meaning to it and thereby allow the Lord to replace our own worldview with a hallowed, sanctified worldview. Responding in this way initiates a process of sanctification that allows us to join the heavenly choirs singing praises. Or, as Nephi elsewhere put it, it allows us to "speak with the tongue of angels and shout praises unto the Holy One of Israel" (2 Nephi 31:13). On the other hand, an inadequate response to revelation would be to hear only passively what the Lord reveals and to remain stuck in our own vain worldview without questioning it. By doing so, we engage in a carnal, sinful way of living and seeing that finally leads us to be "ashamed" of doing what is right, to mock at that which is holy, and last of all, "to fall away."

The Missing Medium: Rereading Revelation as Interruption in 1 Nephi 1

Benjamin Peters

WHAT IS REVELATION? How does one receive it? If revelation can be understood as a divine process for disclosing or manifesting what was previously hidden or unknown, then in what way can we modern readers receive the text of the Book of Mormon—but not the golden plates that revealed them? How, if at all, are we to read this book in light of the fact that the Book of Mormon is a message missing its original medium? This essay seeks in the text of 1 Nephi 1 a fresh reframing and rethinking of these questions. It advances the thesis that we should understand revelation itself as a form of interruption. The essay's argument has three parts: a reading of the text, a comment on two forms of revelation (the *saying* and the *said*), and a few concluding speculations.[1]

---

1. I wish to thank James Faulconer, George Handley, Brian Hauglid, John Durham Peters, Amit Pinchevski, Shirley Ricks, Julie M. Smith, Joseph Spencer, Michaël Ulrich, Miranda Wilcox, and others for their comments and conversations.

Text

Let us begin with a puzzle. What do the following events have in common?

- the coming Babylonian destruction of Jerusalem
- the dislocation of Lehi's vision from outside of Jerusalem to his home
- Nephi's remarkable textual self-consciousness as an author
- Lehi's visionary encounter with the "one" who gives him a book
- the originally intended order of the books in the Book of Mormon
- Martin Harris's loss of the book of Lehi
- Joseph Smith's translation of the plates by looking away from them

The answer, as is probably already obvious, is that in each example revelation appears in the form of an interruption—that is, revelation appears as a divine indirection that disrupts our lives and compels us to take another hard look. The following section chronicles these and other textual moments of interest in 1 Nephi 1 that prompt the reader to do exactly that.

The Book of Mormon begins as remarkably as any work of modern scripture—namely, the first four verses arrest modern readers' sensibilities with the specificity of claims to authorship, chronology, location, and purpose. A fair portion of ancient scripture—such as Genesis and the Gospels, save Luke—employs an omniscient third-person narrator that strands at sea any historical-critical scholarly search for an anchor as fast as that provided by 1 Nephi 1:1–4. Millennia intervene between modern readers and the original texts. The Book of Mormon, appearing in a surge of revelatory translation, disrupts that tradition from its first note—and that note is a veritable power chord of clarity.

First Nephi 1 bursts forth declaring its first-person author—"I Nephi" (v. 1)—who adds five distinct claims about his authorship in the heading and first three verses: (1) The heading finishes with the third-person claim that "this is according to the hand of Nephi," which suddenly shifts without comment into (2) a direct, first-person claim to authorship: "I Nephi wrote this record" (heading). (3) Verse 1 concludes with another potent first-person claim: "Therefore I make a record," which refers to Nephi having inscribed the plates by hand as well as his having quite possibly fashioned them metallurgically. Then verse 3 doubles Nephi's claim of the records he makes "to be true," according to the earliest translated text, by underscoring both the ontological and epistemological processes of making a record: (4) "I make it with mine own hand," and (5) "I make it according to my knowledge."

These five claims amount to a surprisingly self-conscious initial defense of Nephi's relationship to the plates; indeed, it is not until 1 Nephi 9:3 that the reader encounters a more conventional justification of scripture, when Nephi claims, "I have received a commandment of the Lord that I should make these [small] plates." It seems that Nephi, writing as king of his people, clearly understands his role as self-conscious author from the outset but comes to understand his role as revelator only with time (and I know of no work that clarifies how much time that may have been, although it is likely not much).

In 1 Nephi 1:4, Nephi further anchors his narrative in startlingly specific coordinates of person, place, and time—namely, "Lehi," who is "in Jerusalem" during "the first year of the reign of Zedekiah." This verse situates the narrative in relation to two themes coursing throughout Nephi's life and work: the problem of sustaining political kingship in a particular space paired with the problem of sustaining family lineage over time. In particular, verse 4 introduces the parallel between Zedekiah's reign over Judah and King Nephi's reign in the New World, as well as the chronicle stretching from Lehi's Jerusalem to Nephi's failure to hold together his divided family. In order to mark the intersection of these two potent political-theological coordinates, Nephi introduces his father by force of a jarring parenthetical interruption in the syntax of verse 4: "In the commencement of the first year of the reign of Zedekiah, king of Judah (my father, Lehi, having dwelt at Jerusalem in all of his days)."[2]

---

2. Here and occasionally elsewhere I have used my own punctuation in place of that found in Royal Skousen's *The Book of Mormon: The Earliest Text* (New Haven: Yale University Press, 2009).

The book of 1 Nephi arrives in our hands as an already-interrupted book in several other ways. Neither Nephi nor Joseph Smith intended for 1 Nephi to be the first book in the Book of Mormon. Rather, both assumed that the book of Lehi, wherein "[Lehi] hath written many things which he saw in visions and in dreams" (1 Nephi 1:16), would come first. However, because Martin Harris lost the 116-page translation of the book of Lehi in 1828, the beginning is missing.[3] Even before it can say anything, the modern text of 1 Nephi 1 finds itself out of joint, now launching the very narrative—Lehi's story—its author meant only to continue.

Joseph Smith's translation of 1 Nephi 1 also outlines an interrupted process; namely, the loss of the book of Lehi appears to have delayed Joseph Smith from translating 1 and 2 Nephi until after he had successfully translated from Mosiah to Mormon (Joseph translated the Words of Mormon last). Whatever the reader's preferred explanation for the prominence of 1 Nephi 1 (for example, divine foreknowledge is plausibly hinted at in 1 Nephi 9:5: "The Lord hath commanded me to make these plates for a wise purpose in him, which purpose I know not"), we may observe that to assume it was foreknown that the book of Lehi would go missing is also to diagnose the profound self-consciousness the record brings to itself as a translated record in particular and as a record of any shape or form.

The story of Lehi speaking the words of a book received from a heavenly messenger foreshadows the revelatory process by which Joseph Smith would translate the plates he received from the earth under angelic guidance. The interrupted quality of Lehi's first vision resembles Joseph Smith's visionary translation of the plates: both angelic messengers give young founding prophets books to read, and only after some expectant waiting period (the "one" in 1 Nephi 1:9 stands mute before Lehi for an unspecified period, and Joseph waits from 1823 to 1827 before receiving the plates). For all who struggle to read the Book of Mormon, it is suggestive that the book itself, both in

---

3. If organized chronologically, the Book of Mormon would feature the book of Ether first, might then reference the record of the Mulekites, and only then begin the Lehite and Nephite prophetic traditions.

the text and as a translation, begins with a story about readers caught off guard.

It is also curious that, with the exceptions of the grounding points of the rock under the pillar of fire and his bed, Lehi's first vision refuses to stay still: the man initially is moved by "many prophets" (1 Nephi 1:4) to leave the temple in Jerusalem to pray, repent, and offer up a burnt sacrifice on a stone altar "in behalf of his people" (v. 5). There he experiences a vision, wherein he is visited by "a pillar of fire" that "dwelt upon a rock before him" (v. 6), suggesting both an amplified sacrificial altar as well as the sentinel of clouds and fire by which the Lord led Moses and the children of Israel out of ancient Egypt. Lehi, overwhelmed by whatever it is that he "saw and heard" (v. 6), then dislocates his vision by returning to his house at Jerusalem, where he casts himself upon his bed, "overcome with the Spirit," and is then "carried away in a vision" (see vv. 7–8). Lehi's first vision thus appears as a single experience broken across two sites: first, his vision of the pillar of fire was presumably outside the city, and second, his throne theophany was presumably on his bed. The divided first vision leads to the eventual consequence of disrupting and then rending his family as they depart into the wilderness and sail to the New World, but not until Lehi himself interrupts their migration to send his sons to Jerusalem twice, each time for a different means of sustaining lineages: first scriptures and then spouses. In Nephi's retrospective retelling of his divided family, Laman and Lemuel do not complain about the return trip for spouses, although they do complain about Nephi's preoccupation with scripture.

The earliest incident in 1 Nephi 1, Lehi's first vision, is remarkable for the sort of swell of senses that redirects both Lehi and the reader away from the source of an ecstatic vision and toward vocalizing or saying of a "book" (1 Nephi 1:11). Lehi begins by ostensibly leaving Jerusalem's borders where, kneeling before the pillar of fire, he "saw and heard much" (v. 6), but without beholding or listening to anything Nephi saw fit to report. Next, exhausted in his bed, Lehi is "overcome" and begins experiencing a vision literally—that is, visually—as he first "saw the heavens open" (v. 8) and then faces the blindingly bright "luster" of the "one" (v. 9); the visual overstimulation of the vision is owed not only to the light being brighter than the sun but also to its possible timing at night, when Lehi, in bed, would have witnessed the nocturnal pillar of fire that appeared by night to Moses in Egypt. So bright is the light that Lehi appears not to have a full command of his other senses: Nephi reports that Lehi only "thought" (v. 8) he saw God sitting on the throne. Lehi also appears to see without hearing "numberless concourses of angels," who were only "in the attitude" (v. 8), or the visible posture, of praising and singing. It is only after the "one" stands before him, saying nothing at all, that it becomes plausible that Lehi may not be able to hear anything.

Perhaps unable to hear, Lehi is invited to read instead. "Overcome," Lehi has an expectation of conversation that is broken by the "one" handing him a book. The "one" redirects this mute "visionary man," as Lehi later calls himself (1 Nephi 5:4), to a book that Lehi, as a learned Jew, can read out loud. Receiving a book in vision redirects Lehi's attention away from what I will call in a moment the *saying* of conversation and toward the reading of the *said* record. As was common for his time and place, Lehi probably did not subvocalize or read silently. To read a text was to vocalize, or to convert symbols that can be seen on the space of a page into sounds with a voice, a process that takes time. Only in the cognitively demanding act of reading do sight, audition, and vocalization combine in the culminating moment in which Nephi reports that Lehi "*read[s], saying ...*" His utterance "woe woe unto Jerusalem, for I have *seen* thine abominations" (1 Nephi 1:13) gives his own voice, breath, or spirit to the Hebrew consonants or Egyptian hieroglyphs that likely populate the page. (Though, if Joseph Smith is taken as precedent, perhaps Lehi was translating from a language he could not himself have read.) Only by the disciplined act of sounding out his reading of the book is Lehi not "overcome" with the Spirit as before but, instead, is "filled with the Spirit of the Lord" (v. 12). Once well received, the Spirit empowers him not only to see but to hear, and thus to speak and write; that is, not only to receive but to speak revelation as well. His first vision is not a conversation, however. There is no give and take. Lehi talks *to*—not *with*—the "one" by praising him (see v. 14).

The sensory shift in Lehi's vision may be compared to that of the prophet in Isaiah 6: in Isaiah, only by touching to his lips the hot coal given to him can the prophet not only "hear" but "understand," not only "see" but "perceive," and "understand with [his] heart and convert, and be healed" (Isaiah 6:9–10). Only by receiving a book can Lehi shift from hearing to understanding, seeing to perceiving, beholding the "one" to uttering to others a message of destruction. In particular, only after reading and seeing can Lehi vocally "exclaim" unto the Lord (see 1 Nephi 1:14). And only by vocalizing the word does Lehi manage to snap out of ecstatic rapture and into action. If one grants, as some rabbis claim, that the hot coal in Isaiah 6:6–7 is a metaphor for scripture, what begins as a vision ends, for both Isaiah and Lehi, with a purification of the physical body by way of a revelatory text.

Many questions remain about the sensory denouement of Lehi's vision. Was Lehi's utterance a quotation, a translation, or a gloss of the book he read? What book was Lehi given: a Deuteronomic book of law by which he could infer Jerusalem's sin, a Book of the Living registering their actual sins, an account of the future destruction of Jerusalem, or perhaps even a record of the "many things" (1 Nephi 1:13) Lehi would later transcribe into his own book? The text cannot answer these questions, for Nephi interrupts in verse 16 to report that, since his own record is limited, he must abridge his father's account.

Stirred by the prophets, Lehi seeks and finds his own revelation, but rather than conversing with the "one," he disciplines his own overwhelmed senses into the vocal-literate register of the ancient literate scholar, whose importance Nephi showcases in verse 2 as "the language of my father, which consists of the learning of the Jews and the language of the Egyptians." Lehi's first vision may model the kind of revelatory reading by which Joseph Smith would translate the Book of Mormon, receiving revelation from a book that has left, for us, no material trace, but whose presence was enough to prompt the "seer" to speak what he read. In other words, Lehi's vision offers a case study in learning how to receive revelation by indirection. Lehi's experience suggests how we might all understand that reading a book given to us from heaven is a revelatory act—revelation that may at first exhaust our senses before pointing us in new and surprising directions. As Lehi's vision shows, revelation does not turn our attention only to what God and his prophets may yet say; rather, God stands before us waiting patiently for us to read what has already been said. Revelation arrives in ways we may not be ready to receive or perceive. Perhaps to receive revelation is also to speak it; that is, perhaps by interpreting what he read, Lehi began his own process of revelation by interruption.

By interruption I mean any form of divine indirection that disrupts an ongoing message and at once interjects another message in its place. Revelation, like interruption, disrupts our old habits and at once interjects new meaning into our lives. If, in fact, revelation is to have meaning, it must disrupt our lives, unbinding the past and opening new possibilities. First Nephi 1 suggests that revelation also often comes by way of interruption: not only the message but the media that reveal messages do so by means and to effects few can anticipate. For Lehi and for us, revelation suspends our sense of the everyday and in the process reanimates what once appeared ordinary. In structure, historical context, storyline, translation process, and syntax, revelation by interruption is frequent in 1 Nephi 1. Inspiration by indirection is a consistent theme.

Analysis

This section complicates the thesis outlined above by observing that at least two interpenetrating categories of interruption take place in 1 Nephi 1: the revelatory experience of the *saying* and the record keeping of the *said*. Both forms of revelation—what may in the future be said and what has already been said to be revelation—are modeled in the interrupted text, context, structure, and style of 1 Nephi 1. I am borrowing and adapting the terms the *saying* and the *said* from the work of Emmanuel Levinas—among the great twentieth-century philosophers, ethicists, and Talmudic commentators—as well as the media philosopher and Levinas interpreter Amit Pinchevski.[4] I understand the revelatory experience of the *saying* to be a prerational, mystical act of receiving insight, such as an ecstatic vision. And I understand the revealed artifact or rational record based on this saying, such as a book of law, to

---

4. In particular, see Emmanuel Levinas, *Otherwise Than Being or Beyond Essence* (Boston: Kluwer, 1981), and especially Amit Pinchevski, *By Way of Interruption: Levinas and the Ethics of Communication* (Pittsburgh: Duquesne Press, 2005), as well as his recent "Levinas as a Media Theorist: Toward an Ethics of Mediation," *Philosophy and Rhetoric* 47/1 (2014): 48–72.

be the *said*. This distinction is somewhat akin to that of the Dionysian and Apollonian in Western thought and literature. The *saying*, in my reworking of Levinas's terminology, is that which opens oneself to another being in a preoriginal, personal, ecstatic (as in out-of-body, not joyous) experience. The *said*, on the other hand, closes, contains, concretizes, and publicizes the relationship between that saying and the recipient. Thinkers from Moses to Plato to Spinoza to Derrida have dwelled on the complicated role of the prophet in oral and literate cultures as the mouthpiece and the scribe of the Lord. By contrast, the moral teachers from Socrates to Jesus to Confucius, all literate, left the writing of their teachings to their students. Suffice it to observe here that the *sayings* of the Spirit scramble and open the senses in the theophanies of Moses and Lehi, while the *said* revelation of stone tablets and brass plates fixes and regulates the traditions that follow those same prophets.

At first glance, 1 Nephi 1 balances both forms of revelation. The *saying* appears in the form of Lehi's first vision as an ecstatic and overwhelming event in need of interpretation (Nephi offers only that he "saw and heard much"), while the *said* appears in Nephi's record and today in the text of the Book of Mormon itself as a planned, abridged, and already-extant interpretation of the plates. The whole chapter is framed by Nephi's deep anxiety about record keeping, about preserving the *said*, writings so important the Spirit constrains him as a young man in the Old World to kill for them (4:5–19) and, as a mature king in the New World, to live for them.

These distinct senses of revelation also interpenetrate one another. For Nephi, the golden plates are not just the static, fixed *said*. For him, the embodied experience of having personally inscribed and possibly fashioned the plates is no less a part of the revelatory process. The experience of revelatory writing renders the plates true for Nephi. In other words, in verses 1–3, Nephi is literally saying the *said*. His self-consciousness as an author becomes a plain witness of his own firsthand experience of the act of making records. Now consider the content of Nephi's first record: Lehi's overwhelming encounter with the pillar of fire and his sublime and terrible discovery of the city's coming destruction. This revelation is no simple, ecstatic receiving of the *saying*—new heavenly content—for it culminates and in fact cannot be received until Lehi too can be caught saying the *said*, this time by reading a book out loud. As verse 12 pithily puts the peak moment: "He read, saying..." This is not just the son writing what his father said; rather, Nephi writes his record (the *said*) about revelations (the *sayings*) the father read in other records (another *said*). Reading and writing and speaking and saying are bound up in one another. In these few verses, Nephi cannot say all that has been said (he abridges his father's record) because he personally says the *said* by inscribing and fashioning the plates firsthand. Similarly, Lehi cannot hear the "one" speaking to him until he too says the *said* by reading out loud a record received in vision.

This is the key theme: revelation comes by the various combinations of the *saying* and the *said*. By speaking out loud the records until we can speak for ourselves and by experiencing the writing of records firsthand, by reading ecstatically and by speaking forth records, our own lives can be interrupted by revelations. To capture this dual nature of the *saying/said* revelation, Lehi and Nephi offer in 1 Nephi 1 a new image that is a companion to the hot coal of the prophet in Isaiah 6, the burning bush of Moses in Exodus, and other images for deep texts as fires in Jewish thought—namely, Lehi's "pillar of fire," whose dynamic flame of inspiration dances upon the rock of recorded revelation.

Conclusion

The reading and analysis offered thus far have speculated about how we might understand revelation as interruption. As outlined in this reading of 1 Nephi 1, the call to receive revelation by and as interruption is no lesser standard. It is, if anything, a more challenging mode of revelation. After all, no one likes to be interrupted, except by the answers we already seek. And revelation, if it is to change us, must continually interrupt our lives. To expect otherwise is folly. Yet real comfort awaits in the sustainable scramble that is a revelation-lit life. As John attributes the words to Christ, "Nevertheless I tell you the truth; It is expedient for you that I go away: for if I go not away, the Comforter will not come unto you; but if I depart, I will send him unto you" (John 16:7). Our missing media give us cause to celebrate the stubbornly good news that is contemporary revelation: we do not and cannot possess all that has been said, and because of that fact there remains much left to do and say. To that end, three thoughts follow: a note on reading, a note on revelation, and a note on the missing golden plates.

First, the text of 1 Nephi 1 reveals what was too obvious to notice: 1 Nephi 1 is quite possibly the most overread and underexamined chapter in Latter-day Saint scripture. I am not alone among the modern readers of the Book of Mormon who have overlooked the lesson of revelatory interruption in it: after hearing about the two-week seminar behind this volume, a friend joked that she had spent far longer reading and rereading 1 Nephi 1, and in her estimation, to less effect. Between the children, the calendars, and the callings that fill our lives, we return to the book again and again like Lehi at first "hearing and seeing much" without having much to say for it, wondering when we will experience the record anew. Sometimes the best we can get is a pale imitation of revelation by interruption—namely, opening to a page at random and pointing.

But revelation by the pillar of fire promises more. For Lehi, Nephi, and the modern reader alike, the experience of revelatory reading begins with the repentant recognition that the revelation we seek is not absent, carried away to some distant, more glorious, and more real realm, but that it awaits us, hidden in plain view in front of us. It awaits our saying of the *said*, in the interpretive labor and adventure that is reading first what a text has actually said and then for what it is saying to us here and now.

We may reenvision our own New World heroes in this light: Nephi may be less a muscle-bound paladin hero than he is a displaced Jewish scholar preoccupied with sealing his broken family with a record. He offers a learned bridge to a literary tradition, practicing not faith in written words but the written words of his faith. Nephi may be a fertile "foreign founder," in Bonnie Honig's phrase, in terms of his literary heirs—the end of the transmission of his family lineage and the launching of a tradition of New World reading and writing of records, one the modern readership of the Book of Mormon would do well to consider inheriting and likening to ourselves.[5]

---

5. Bonnie Honig, *Democracy and the Foreigner* (Princeton: Princeton University Press, 2003).

Second, 1 Nephi 1 compels us to rethink the nature of revelation. Understood as interruption, the revelation of *saying* must always unfold before us (it can only be contemporary), while the records of what has been *said* provide bedrock upon which the stakes of Zion may be built. The mutual interruption of the *said* and the *saying* takes us in revelatory directions that we by definition cannot expect—especially when that direction is to not move at all. A spiritually alert life may rest on the learned capacity to find a gap—and there are many—and then to learn from it. The text's abundant silences, lapses, and unanswered queries are not the bugs but the features of the human condition that open us for revelation.

If Lehi must look away from the "one" before he can read the heavenly book; if Nephi had to self-consciously abridge his record of his father; if Lehi can forget both scriptures and spouses on his way into the desert; and if Joseph had to look away from the golden plates before he could speak forth the words of the Book of Mormon, then we too need not fret when we sometimes receive unexpected messages by way of unanticipated media. It is folly to imagine, as I note below, that we can discover the golden plates as ancient historians and archaeologists might hope—not because it could not happen, but because it would not be revelation if it did. So too are our expectations dashed ever revealingly, if we will but look, against the interruptions of daily life. When we expect to find an answer in the scriptures, revelation may await us in prayer. When we expect the answer to come in prayer, it may await in the spark of a text. Perhaps no truth can be received and confirmed at once; the completion of revelation—because both the *said* and the *saying* overwhelm the present moment—is ever postponed.

This is not only a feature of divine revelation but is also a fixture of our lot as limited, learning, mortal revelators. To say, with a nod to Malachi 3:10, that the heavens have more revelation in store for us than we are prepared to receive is not only to genuflect to the superabundance of heavenly wisdom but is also to recognize our finite capacity to register, process, receive, store, retrieve, and act on revelation by interruption. This is not to place blame for our mortal toils on the imperfect language, texts, and media that stand between mortals and the divine. It is, instead, to celebrate the good news that there will always be more to receive and to say.

Finally, a note on the missing medium of the golden plates. The media theorist and wordsmith Marshall McLuhan once memorably advised that before visiting Russia, the first thing a foreigner should know is that there are no phonebooks in Moscow. His immediate point was that a visitor should have social networks in place before arriving in Russia because Russia works by way of its interpersonal networks. But his larger point was, as it is here, that sometimes it is the missing medium that tells us the most. The same can be said of the missing medium behind the Book of Mormon. It is self-evident that the golden plates are not present and cannot be examined. The thing that matters most about these absent plates, however, is not the instinct that shipwrecks scholars in pursuit of the artifactual origins of the Book of Mormon. The absent plates cannot be what matters most because, by divine indirection, we have no material medium, no golden plates to behold, and no original record to scrutinize.

Moreover, if we insist on examining the Book of Mormon only as a means for indexing truth claims that are external to the book, we risk repeating the very mistaken model of revelation that the Book of Mormon compels us to discard. Revelation cannot be the uncovering of the more original, the more authentic, or the more immediate communion with the mind of God because revelation works by way of interruptions. The text models this. In almost every detail, the text suspends the search for the lost medium and instead asks us to work on the message. Now, I am not suggesting we should wholly ignore the fact that the Book of Mormon is missing its source text. Rather, we need to acknowledge that the missing medium is the necessary port from which to embark on a journey sure to proceed by way of revelatory interruptions.

As outlined above, 1 Nephi 1 models how modern readers might respond to the fact that the message is missing its original medium. Like Lehi standing mute before his open vision, like Nephi seeking to extend his heritage with a record, and like Joseph translating plates by peering into a hat, perhaps we too begin to "receive" the message of the Book of Mormon only after first looking away from the medium. The missing medium may lure some readers to search for its imprint or counterproof in Mesoamerican archaeology or ancient history, but once we understand revelation as interruption, we cannot miss the presence of the far greater, if sometimes unbearably mundane, medium that ever interrupts our search for the missing medium: the text of the book itself. It is in working patiently through the specifics of the text that we uncover what was always the already-available revelation, a translated text awaiting the redeeming labor of reading.

Contributors

GEORGE B. HANDLEY is professor of interdisciplinary humanities and associate dean of the College of Humanities at Brigham Young University. He has published widely in comparative studies of literature of the Americas and in environmental humanities. He is also the author of the environmental memoir, *Home Waters: A Year of Recompenses on the Provo River* (University of Utah Press, 2010). He and his wife, Amy, are the parents of four children and live in Provo.

ADAM S. MILLER is a professor of philosophy at Collin College in McKinney, Texas. He earned a PhD in philosophy from Villanova University. He is the author of six books, including *Letters to a Young Mormon* (Neal A. Maxwell Institute, 2014), *The Gospel according to David Foster Wallace* (Bloomsbury, 2016), and *Future Mormon* (Greg Kofford Books, 2016). He directs the Mormon Theology Seminar and coedits a series of books for the Maxwell Institute entitled Groundwork: Studies in Theory and Scripture.

BENJAMIN PETERS is associate professor of media studies at the University of Tulsa and affiliated faculty at the Information Society Project at Yale Law School. He is author of *How Not to Network a Nation: The Uneasy History of the Soviet Internet* (MIT Press, 2016) and editor of *Digital Keywords: A Vocabulary of Information Society and Culture* (Princeton University Press, 2016). His work site is benjaminpeters.org.

JULIE M. SMITH graduated from the University of Texas at Austin with a BA in English and from the Graduate Theological Union in Berkeley, California, with an MA in biblical studies. She is on the executive board of the Mormon Theology Seminar and the steering committee for the BYU New Testament Commentary, for which she is writing a commentary on the Gospel of Mark. She is the author of *Search, Ponder, and Pray: A Guide to the Gospels* (Greg Kofford Books, 2014). Julie is married to Derrick Smith; they live near Austin, Texas, where she homeschools their three children. She also blogs for Times & Seasons, where she is the book review editor.

JOSEPH M. SPENCER earned his PhD from the University of New Mexico and is currently visiting assistant professor in the Department of Ancient Scripture at Brigham Young University. He is the author of three books: *For Zion* (Greg Kofford Books, 2014), *An Other Testament* (Neal A. Maxwell Institute, 2016), and most recently, *The Vision of All: Twenty-Five Lectures on Isaiah in Nephi's Record* (Greg Kofford Books, 2016). He serves as the associate director of the Mormon Theology Seminar and is the editor of the *Journal of Book of Mormon Studies*. He and Karen, his wife, live in Provo, Utah, with their five children.

MICHAËL ULRICH has been a PhD student in mathematics at Université de Franche-Comté (France) and at Ernst-Moritz-Arndt-Universität Greifswald (Germany) until June 2016. He graduated from the Ecole Normale Supérieure (Paris campus) in January 2015. Besides his mathematical interests, he devotes his free time to Mormon studies.

MIRANDA WILCOX is associate professor of English at Brigham Young University in Provo, Utah, where she teaches medieval literature. Her research focuses on the intersections of religious and textual culture in early medieval Europe, particularly in Anglo-Saxon England. She coedited *Standing Apart: Mormon Historical Consciousness and the Concept of Apostasy* (Oxford University Press, 2014).